Little
While
Times

Triumph Through Tough Times

By
Pastor Jim Combs
Dr. Randy T. Johnson

Published by:
Rochester Media, Inc
PO Box 80002
Rochester, MI 48308
248-429-READ (7323)
248-430-8799 fax
info@rochestermedia.com
www.rochestermedia.com

All scripture quotations, unless otherwise indicated, are taken from Holy Bible, English Standard Version 2001

Author:Pastor Jim Combs & Dr. Randy Johnson
Cover Design: Julius deChavez
Formating by Brian Jamieson - www.jamiesondesign.net

First U.S. Edition Year 1ˢᵗ Edition was Published
Summary: Little While Times
ISBN: 978-1468148909

1.Christian Living, Spiritual Growth, Christianity, Religion

For current information about releases by Dr. Randy Johnson or other releases from Rochester Media, visit our website: http://www.rochestermedia.com

Little While Times

Triumph Through Tough Times

By
Pastor Jim Combs
Dr. Randy T. Johnson

Table of Contents

Introduction

It is comforting to experience that you don't have to be an expert to succeed. Pastor Jim got a buck his very first time deer hunting. He wasn't in his prearranged location, he hadn't shot the gun before, and his only bait was a Twinkie wrapper that he had dropped. He didn't realize until later how amazing of an experience that was.

It is not so comforting to realize that it is difficult to succeed in life. We will go through difficult times. These times don't have to be because of wrong choices or even personal failure. It is just that life can get pretty interesting some days. It is those days that we might not like what we are or even who we are. Those times are SMH days – shake my head days - days we wonder what has happened.

In John 16, Jesus is talking to His disciples. He says, "A little while, and ye shall not see me; and again, a little while, and ye shall see me,

because I go to the Father" (verse 16). Jesus loves His disciples and He is trying to prepare them. The timing is right before He is sold and crucified. It is right before their whole world would be turned around. They had to be wondering, "What is this not see you, see you stuff." They were understandably confused.

Theologians have also wondered the meaning

of Jesus' words. Was He referring to His death and resurrection or was he referring to His second coming? Either way, the disciples were going to face the worst day of their lives.

It may seem obvious that the death of Jesus was the worst day of their lives, but it was even more unnatural for them. They were all Jewish boys. They were looking for the Messiah who would bring in a new kingdom. They were sure that Jesus would be ushered in as the new king. The Jews would be released from the bondage of the Romans. They would have a King and a kingdom. And then, all their dreams were crushed in one day. These are the little while times.

Jesus said that in a "little while" they would not see Him. That little while didn't feel so little to them. They realized that they had betrayed Him, disappointed Him, deserted Him and even denied Him. They watched their dreams die on the cross.

Everyone will face "little while times." The reality is that you are either just coming out of a little while time, in the midst of one, or about to enter one. Worse yet, it may be a combination where you are just coming out of one bad period to enter another. It is those times we ask sincere questions: How did I get here? I loved her. Why did she leave? How am I going to make my house payment? What should I do now that I have received a phone call that my child has been arrested? It is a lonely time, a lonely night, when you are discouraged and just can't sleep.

It is helpful to realize that all our heroes had little while times. They all experienced times with which they wished they wouldn't have to deal. This book is a reminder that the little while time of Jesus' death became known as Good Friday. It was a good event for us as the Savior died for our sins. Easter Sunday seemed ions away, but it completed the scenario, bringing hope of eternal life. Your life might be stuck on a little while time of a Friday, but, with the right response and attitude, Sunday is coming.

Let's look at some heroes of Scripture and see how they responded to little while times. It will give us a map to victory.

Chapter 1

Bitter Sweet

"Now it came to pass in the days when the judges ruled, that there was a famine in the land. And a certain man of Bethlehem in Judah went to sojourn in the country of Moab, he, and his wife, and his two sons" (Ruth 1:1). The story follows that Elimelech is married to Naomi and they have two sons named Mahlon and Chilion. Chilion is one cool name. You could just call him "Chill." However, things weren't very chill in Bethlehem as there was a famine. Many can relate to Elimelech. There is no work. You wonder how you will make the house payment. You are given repossession papers. You struggle to get simple

It is the wrong order. Parents shouldn't have to bury their children.

things like shoes for your kids. You are just trying to figure out how to make it. Elimelech hears things are better across the river. So, being a man who will do anything to take care of his family, he moves with them to Moab.

In Moab, tragedy strikes. Elimelech dies.

They have moved away from family and friends, and their husband and dad dies. The boys know their position and responsibility and step up to take care of the family. Both boys marry girls of Moab: Orpah and Ruth. They had their festive Jewish weddings. There would have been food, music and celebration. Things were picking up. They stayed there 10 years, making it their home. Then, tragedy strikes again. Both Mahlon and Chilion (whose names, ironically, mean sick and weak) die. Naomi has already buried her husband and now has to bury both sons. It is not supposed to be this way. It is the wrong order. Parents shouldn't have to bury their children. Besides the grieving and depression, Naomi can't meet the needs.

Naomi decides to go back to Bethlehem. Israel had a welfare system where farmers would leave the corners of their fields for orphans, widows and those who couldn't make ends meet. She encourages her daughters-in-law to go find husbands and start over. Orpah  takes the advice, but Ruth refuses to leave Naomi alone with a beautiful commitment, "whither thou goest, I will go; and where thou lodgest, I will lodge: thy people shall be my people, and thy God my God" (Ruth 1:16). The two ladies head back to Bethlehem.

As Naomi enters the land, the people greet her warmly. Naomi's name means sweetness, which probably gives us an insight into her character and personality. We remember sweet people. They are the ones who brighten up a room as they enter. People want to be around them. Naomi was sweetness, but, as she is met by the people, she informs them that her name has changed: "And she said unto them, Call me not Naomi, call me Mara; for the Almighty hath dealt very bitterly with me" (Ruth 1:20). Mara means bitter. Naomi has changed her name from sweetness to bitter. She is basically saying her sweetness is gone. Joy has been ripped from her soul. She has been and is going through tough times. Her little while times seem too long and too painful. She is a bitter, angry, hurt woman. Most know the feeling. The smile has been knocked off your face. The joy is ripped out of your heart. You are defeated. It often comes from places that weren't expected. We are left asking how this happened to us.

Nevertheless, Naomi and Ruth are in Bethlehem. Naomi sends Ruth out to collect from the corners of the fields. While there, Ruth is noticed by the landowner. He takes an interest in her and respects her humble spirit. This landowner, Boaz, offers her water and encourages his workers to leave more grain for her. It appears he might have a crush on her and is flirting. The initial introduction turns into one of the greatest love stories in the Bible. They have their courtship, marriage and eventually even a son. The start of Ruth 4:17 says, "And the women, her neighbors, gave him a name, saying, There is a son born to Naomi; and they called his name Obed." It was common in the Hebrew to refer to the grandmother as the mother of her grandson, especially a widow with no sons. That isn't the most interesting part of the phrase. The shocker is that they again

refer to her as Naomi, not Mara. Naomi has gone from sweetness to bitterness and is now back to sweetness. She has survived her little while time. She is no longer bitter, but better. But, how did this happen?

Verse 17 says that they named the son Obed. The intriguing part is that Obed means "to serve." This is the advice needed for a culture that is so self-centered. When we invest and focus on helping others, then we will find ourselves being fixed. People need to realize that there are those who have it worse than them. The well-known but anonymous plaque is so powerful, "I complained I didn't have shoes, until I saw the man with no feet." It appears Naomi got her sweetness back through service.

The world wants to steal your joy. You will have little while times. The remedy is to get an Obed. This doesn't mean have a child. It means find a person to invest in. Make a difference in someone's life. Do it intentionally.

It is beautiful to see all of verse 17, "And the women, her neighbors, gave him a name, saying, There is a son born to Naomi; and they called his name Obed; he is the father of Jesse, the father of David." Obed has a son named Jesse, who has a son named David, who is the lineage of another son born in Bethlehem named Jesus. When little while times come, choose to serve. Find an Obed to serve and invest in. This one led to a king and even the King of Kings.

Are you going through a little while time? Did you receive a bad report from your doctor? Find some body to invest in.

1. Pray now for insight to notice that someone God has placed in your life.

2. What name comes to mind? Is there more than one?

3. When will you contact them?

4. How will you encourage and serve them?

Picture of Brick Cross by Keoni Cabral

"A successful man is one who can lay a firm foundation
with the bricks others have thrown at him."
David Brinkley

Chapter 2

"Get Thee Up"

"I am not a religious man." Does that phrase bother you? This book is built on the foundation that a real God sent His real Son to a real people so we can have a real relationship with that real God. The emphasis is on a relationship, not a religion. Not only is it about relationship, but it is based on a real God. This chapter is a reminder that God is real. The relationship is based on mutual communication.

Jesus told his disciples that in a "little while" he would be gone, and in a "little while" he would be back. Seeing how characters of the Bible got through these little while times can be helpful. However, in this study, we will be challenged with a harsh reality. The truth is that most of our little while times were brought  on by ourselves. Most little while times were created out of bad choices, bad decisions.

Joshua chapter 7 contains a Bible hero creating his own little while time. Moses has already died, so God's people are being led into Israel by

Joshua. Chapters 5 and 6 describe one of the biggest
victories of all time as God's people defeat Jericho.
Jericho didn't fear anyone, as they had walls that
were 30 feet high and 12 feet thick. The walls were
so thick that apartments were built within them and
chariot races were run on them. The defense was
mammoth. However, nothing is too difficult for
God. So, within the week, "Joshua fit the battle of
Jericho, and the walls came tumbling down."

Ai is the next city. It is nothing compared to
Jericho. Ai is so small that it is always referred to as
being near another city. It isn't large enough to stand
alone. In Joshua chapter 7, Joshua sends out scouts
(verse 2). The report came back that there were no
walls, no army and no problem. So, Joshua only sent
3,000 men. He didn't send the whole army. Verse 5
says that the men of Ai smote them and killed 36
men. God's people didn't lose anyone to Jericho, but
lost 36 to Ai. It didn't make sense.

Joshua gives his response to the loss in verse
7, "And Joshua said, Alas, O LORD God, wherefore
hast thou at all brought this people over Jordan, to
deliver us into the hand of the Amorites, to destroy
us? Would to God we had been content, and dwelt on
the other side Jordan!" He just saw the walls come
down, and now he whines and says that maybe they
should have stayed and been content wandering. He
thought he would have an easy victory, but now he
goes through a little while time. Joshua is broken;
things didn't turn out as he thought. Sometimes this
world will disappoint us.

In Joshua 7:10, God gives the pivotal command, "Get thee up." God takes Joshua through a recovery process of basically 5 steps. Several statements can be implied by the simple phrase, "Get thee up."

1.   Stop Whining!

Why are believers known as the biggest whiners in the world? What do we have to whine about? What good has it done us? How has whining made anything better? Has whining fixed your marriage? Has whining about your children done anything for them? Has whining about our country helped? Has whining about the church done anything good for anyone? We act like spoiled rotten babies.

There is something important we need to realize. If you know Jesus Christ as your personal Savior and everything in your life goes bust, you are still ahead in the game. You still win. Besides having a future in Heaven, we still have a bed, food, transportation… Do we deserve this or is it the grace of God?

If you know Jesus Christ as your personal savior and everything in your life goes bust, you are still ahead in the game. You still win.

A common complaint in the church today is that the world doesn't want our message. We need to remember that Paul took the Gospel to towns who didn't want it. He was beaten and put in prison. The towns he went to didn't have "In God we Trust" on their currency. He went to towns that didn't have any converts. He went, he made a difference and he didn't pout. Actually, he even sang praises while in prison. We need to stop whining and "Get thee up."

2.   Take Responsibility!

To stop whining is a good start, but we also need to take responsibility. Joshua needed to take  responsibility for his actions or lack of action. Joshua never asked God once what he should do at Ai. Joshua never went to God. He decided to do it on his own. Joshua was responsible for those 36 guys getting killed. He needed to stop whining and realize he was part of the problem.

We live during a time when people don't want to take responsibility. It is always somebody else's fault. It is the age of the irresponsible generation. Instead of doing the homework, we blame the teacher or the school system. Instead of getting to work on time, we blame our boss for being a jerk. We tend to blame everyone from our parents to our pastors. We have men not paying child support because they are mad at their ex-spouse, and then they blame her. We need to be responsible. Instead of whining, we need to look into a mirror. Where do

I need to take responsibility? I don't have to be the one most responsible to still be challenged to take responsibility for my part.

3. Do something about it!

Taking responsibility may be the cognitive step, but it can't stop there. We need to take action. We need to do something about it! Too many people whine about their marriage and don't do anything about it. Paul Meier has said, "Every couple deserves each other." When you hear someone rip on their spouse, realize they are in essence ripping on themselves. I may feel the majority of the problem is with someone else, but I still need to own up to my part and do something about it. Bluntly put, "Shut up, or do something about it."

4. Get Honest!

Joshua whined and God said, "Israel hath sinned" (verse 11). God was honest. Of course He was. However, people today try to avoid honesty. A drawing card for the mega church movement is that people won't have to hear what they don't want to hear. They will be entertained and receive a feel good message. The reality is, if you regularly attend a church and are

> When the choice comes to pleasing man or God, we need to get honest and please God.

never uncomfortable, then something is probably wrong. Eventually someone has to bring up the topic of sin. Israel had sinned. We, too, struggle with sin. We must identify it.

In Galatians 1, Paul starts off strong: "I marvel that ye are so soon removed from him that called you into the grace of Christ unto another gospel" (verse 6). He says he is amazed at their sin. He tells them they have already moved to another gospel, one that doesn't come from the grace of God - hence, one that doesn't save. This feel-good message is another gospel.

Paul continues in verse 10, "For do I now persuade men, or God? Or do I seek to please men? For if I yet pleased men, I should not be the servant of Christ." Paul says he preaches to an audience of One: God Himself. We need to attend a church where the truth is told, where the preacher says the truth, and where his goal is to please God. When the choice comes to pleasing man or God, we need to get honest and please God.

When little while times come, we need to stop whining, take responsibility, do something about it, get honest, and do what needs to be done.

5.   Do What Needs To Be Done!

The first step in doing what needs to be done is to humble ourselves. We need to admit our faults and sin. We need to stop the excuses and do something productive. Joshua needed to realize that

36 moms were going to be told their sons weren't coming home. He needed to stop his pity party and do something. If he doesn't do something, the boys would have died in vain. Don't go through little while times in vain. Let God take you places only He can. Let God do things only He can.

Listen for God's still, soft voice and Get Thee up!

Picture by Upsilon Andromedae

"Success is falling nine times and getting up ten."
Jon Bon Jovi

Chapter 3

Two Strikes and You're Out

Mount Nebo could qualify for the good, the bad and the ugly category.

Mount Nebo has some good qualities. Mount Nebo is located in the country of Jordan (formerly Moab) and is 2680 feet above sea level. It provides a panorama of the Holy Land. To the south, one can see the Dead Sea. Right across the Dead Sea is where David hid from Saul and wrote some of the Psalms.  The river that flows into the Dead Sea is the Jordan River. This is the same river that John the Baptist spent valuable time in calling all to repentance and in pointing to Jesus. To the north, attached to the Jordan River is the Sea of Galilee where Jesus and Peter later take a walk. Across from Mount Nebo is Jericho. It was kind of an introduction to the first villain for the Israelites. Across the valley are the hills of Judah where David played as a boy as he cared for the sheep. In the distance are the 7 hills of

Jerusalem where Jesus was crucified. It is a beautiful site that is going to start to bring great history for the people of God.

Mount Nebo had an ugly event as we welcomed in the new millennium. On January 1st, 2000, the bombing of Mount Nebo was part of the planned attacks by Osama Bin Laden.

Mount Nebo did have a bad aspect to it. It was probably more of a sad situation for Moses than really a bad one. In Deuteronomy 34, God instructs Moses to climb Mount Nebo. Verse 1 says that God showed Moses all the land. This is the Promised Land. Verse 4 says, "And the LORD said unto him, This is the land which I sware unto Abraham, unto Isaac, and unto Jacob, saying, I will give it unto thy seed; I have caused thee to see it with thine eyes, but thou shalt not go over thither." God reminds Moses that He is keeping His promise He made to Abraham. God shows Moses the land, but also lets him know he won't be allowed to enter the land. God is showing him what he is going to miss. Moses had lead the people of Israel for 40 years, but would not walk in that land. It was a beautiful view of a beautiful land, but he wouldn't get to taste it.

Moses then dies on Mount Nebo. This view of the Promised Land was a segment of his parting moments. This could have been a time of reflecting on the crossing of the Red Sea, or how God had miraculously provided for them with manna and even meat, or how God had sustained their shoes and clothing, but it probably was a time of reflecting on a day he wished he could change. Moses must have thought, "If I could just undo one day in my life. If I could just do one thing different, change one bad moment, change one bad decision." It was one decision that kept Moses out of the Promised Land. He couldn't rewind, undo or erase.

Most of us, if not all of us, have had little while times where we looked back, wishing we  could just change one little thing. We tend to wander back to that one day we wish we could forget. We ache over that one day, or even minute, where our action or inaction caused us years of pain. Moses could relate. Moses had many victories and a scrapbook full of positive times, but that one day stopped him from his ultimate dream and journey.

In Exodus 17, the people of Israel are thirsty and are complaining. They are totally out of hand and Moses is drained. God tells Moses, "Behold, I will stand before thee there upon the rock in Horeb; and thou shalt smite the rock, and there shall come water out of it, that the people may drink. And Moses did so in the sight of the elders of Israel" (verse 6). Moses struck the rock and water came out. It was an amazing miracle, and God let Moses be part of it. This was the ultimate feeling.

So, in Numbers chapter 20 we read that the people are thirsty again, and again are complaining.

Moses turns to God, Who tells him, "Take the rod, and gather thou the assembly together, thou, and Aaron thy brother, and speak ye unto the rock before their eyes; and it shall give forth his water, and thou shalt bring forth to them water out of the rock: so thou shalt give the congregation and their beasts drink" (verse 8). It seems like the same situation, but it isn't. This time God tells Moses to speak unto the rock. He is not to strike it, but just speak to it. In verses 10 and 11, he goes where he wishes he never would have gone. In arrogance, he strikes the rock twice: "And Moses and Aaron gathered the congregation together before the rock, and he said unto them, Hear now, ye rebels; must we fetch you water out of this rock? And Moses lifted up his hand, and with his rod he smote the rock twice; and the water came out abundantly, and the congregation drank, and their beasts also." It is hard to believe that Moses would say, "Must we fetch you water out of this rock?" This was God's work; why would Moses take credit? Furthermore, instead of speaking to the rock, he strikes it twice. Fortunately, God still gave the people water. God cares and provides for His people even in those times we are wrong.

Numbers 20:12 gives the words that end up haunting and affecting Moses until his death, "And the LORD spake unto Moses and Aaron, Because ye believed me not, to sanctify me in the eyes of the children of Israel, therefore ye shall not bring this congregation into the land which I have given them." Because of that disobedient action, Moses would not be allowed to enter the Promised Land.

Sometimes decisions we make during our little while times affect our future. There is no good excuse for disobedience to God. Choices have consequences.

It might seem like God is being a little harsh on Moses. We need to look deeper in Scripture.

1 Corinthians 10:4 says, "And did all drink the same spiritual drink; for they drank of that spiritual Rock that followed them; and that Rock was Christ." Jesus, the Rock of Ages, the One we place our lives on, was the Rock. Verse 2 lets us know that the context is  Moses. The passage speaks of God providing meat and water. This water came from the Rock, Jesus. Moses struck Jesus two times. God could not tolerate this.

The first time Moses struck the rock, it was symbolic of Jesus being smitten. It was a picture of the cross. Jesus had to be smitten so He could give us the water of life. In John 4, Jesus tells the Samaritan woman that anyone who drinks of His water will never thirst again. Moses was to strike the rock the first time. It showed that Jesus' death would give us life. However, the second time he was clearly told to speak to the rock. It would be wrong for Jesus to be crucified a second time.

Hebrews 6:6 says it would bring open shame

on the Son of God, "If they shall fall away, to renew them again unto repentance; seeing they crucify to themselves the Son of God afresh, and put him to an open shame." Striking the Rock the second time was wrong. That was the line that could not be crossed. Once was all that God was going to take. Moses struck the Rock and therefore couldn't go into the Promised Land.

How did Moses get to that point? Most of the problems in our lives we have brought upon ourselves. However, people can hurt people. There are cases where our little while times were caused by someone else. Numbers 20:10 seems to give the reason Moses went too far: "And Moses and Aaron gathered the congregation together before the rock, and he said unto them, Hear now, ye rebels; must  we fetch you water out of this rock?" The people are exercising their well-trained gift of complaining again when Moses calls them rebels. The word rebel is from the same root work that Naomi changed her name to – Mara. Mara means bitter. Rebels refer to bitter makers. Moses calls them bitter makers. It is an interesting word as we know that rebels do make people bitter. In essence, Moses says, "You hurt me."

People will hurt us. The ones that we don't expect it from often hurt the most. The list can go on:

We need to refuse to have bitter makers in our lives.

Parents, friends, lover, children, teacher, neighbor, church, pastor, boss, coach. Don't let them become bitter makers. Don't let yourself get to a point where you look back in regret. We need to refuse to have bitter makers in our lives. When people hurt us, we need to welcome them back. We can't let them steal our joy. We can't let them get the best of us.

When people hurt us, we need to give them to God. We need to be kind to them. We need to love those that hurt us and be kind to those who wrong us.

We need to give them to God so, when we stand on the Mount Nebo of our lives, we will be able to move forward.

Picture by Ed Yourdon

"Most people give up just when they're about to achieve success. They quit on the one yard line. They give up at the last minute of the game one foot from a winning touchdown."

Ross Perot

Chapter 4

Left-handed, Right-minded

Jim Abbott is a hero. It was amazing that he played high school varsity baseball; but it didn't stop there. He went on to play at the University of Michigan, win a gold medal at the 1988 Summer Olympics, play 11 seasons in the Majors, and even throw a no-hitter against the Cleveland Indians. That isn't what made him a hero. He did all those accomplishments without a right hand. He primarily pitched in the American League and due to the Designated Hitter, he didn't have to bat. However, he pitched a little while in the National League where he batted 21 times, and he got 2 hits. Jim Abbott got 2 hits batting one-handed. Where some people see obstacles, heroes see opportunities to amaze. Jim Abbott knew how to overcome a little while time.

You are either going to beat little while times or they are going to beat you.

There are basically 2 kinds of people: those who have had the ability to overcome little while times and those who don't. It doesn't matter if you are male or female, rich or poor, young or mature. You are either going to beat little while times or they are going to beat you.

Judges 20:16 introduces us to 700 men who learned how to overcome little while times; "Among all this people there were seven hundred chosen men lefthanded; every one could sling stones at an hair breadth, and not miss." No other book of the Bible describes someone as left-handed; yet here there are a group of 700. Lefties often take pride in their uniqueness, but this isn't about being better. Lefties weren't always well-received in a culture. Not too long ago, some private schools made students write right-handed. So, being left-handed was not necessarily special.

The only other passage to describe someone as left-handed is also in Judges: "But when the children of Israel cried unto the LORD, the LORD raised them up a deliverer, Ehud the son of Gera, a Benjamite, a man lefthanded: and by him the children of Israel sent a present unto Eglon the king of Moab" (3:15). Ehud was a left-handed judge of Israel. The cycle of Judges is repeated several times through history. First, the people sin - they disobey God. Second, God allows their actions to have consequences - they become enslaved. Third, God's people cry out to God and return to Him. Fourth, God hears the cry and sends a judge, better understood as a hero. God often used people with unusual characteristics as His leader: Samson (strength), Gideon (least in his house), Deborah (woman), Ehud (left-handed).

It seems odd that it would be important to describe Ehud as left-handed.

The story in Judges 3 has Ehud requesting a private meeting with Eglon, king of Moab. He was coming to offer a present. Ehud had strapped to his right thigh a dagger. When everyone else left the room, Ehud pulled out his dagger and thrust it into the belly of the king, killing him (3:21). Ehud is the hero. However,  this raises a question: How does the enemy get a private meeting with the king?

It is possible that Ehud got a private meeting with the king because he was left-handed. It was common for captives to become weakened by their captors so that they couldn't revolt. In 1 Samuel 11:2 we read, "And Nahash the Ammonite answered them, On this condition will I make a covenant with you, that I may thrust out all your right eyes, and lay it for a reproach upon all Israel." Nahash wanted to thrust or gouge out the right eye of every captive. This would bring psychological pain, but also physical disability. Their dominate eye, their aiming eye, would be gone. It would even affect peripheral vision.

Another way to contain captives was to eliminate their right hand. This could either be by cutting it off or just by making it unusable. Ehud probably got his private meeting with the king because he wasn't viewed as a threat. The 700 chosen, left-handed men of Judges 20:16 probably had to overcome a little while time of losing a limb. The passage says they did it well: "Among all this people there were seven hundred chosen men left-handed; every one could sling stones at an hair breadth, and not miss." They could throw a sling to a hair breadth and not miss. They were accurate. The typical weapon was sword and shield, which would take 2 arms. However, they chose a sling, which only takes 1 arm.

These men had patriotic pride. They wanted to be part of the army. They had no right arm and were disabled, but that didn't stop their spirit. Israel's army is known for patriotic pride. America has experienced this same pride. When Pearl Harbor was attacked, the enlistment lines were long. When the Twin Towers were hit, America again came together. When pressure comes, a county comes together. Israel is always under pressure. Even today, every boy and girl automatically serves some time in the military. This is patriotic pride.

Some people have the ability to overcome their little while times and some people do not. These 700 men can teach us 4 characteristics on how to overcome little while times. Don't let little while times overcome you.

1. Be willing to work

When difficulties come, we need to be

willing to work. All too often in America we feel that somebody owes us something. It seems like

The butterfly needs to fight its way out

people are either suing someone or being sued. We need to be willing to work. The butterfly is a good example. When a butterfly is coming out of a cocoon, there is a battle. It is hard work. If someone steps up and cuts open the cocoon, the butterfly will get out easily. The problem is that the butterfly will fall to the ground, never fly and quickly die. The butterfly needs to fight its way out. This fight makes it strong enough to fly. Maybe we don't fly because we don't fight through little while times.

2. Fight through frustrations

These 700 men had to be willing to work. Not only did they try to survive, but they wanted to thrive. They didn't just work to get by, but they kept getting back up. We struggle with brushing our teeth left-handed or writing our name on paper. They took it a lot further by trying to excel at the sling. It would not have been natural. They fought through their frustrations. They didn't give up. They didn't let the circumstances of this world win.

3. Train your eye on the target

These men learned to throw a stone to the breadth of a hair every time. They identified a target and then went after it. Their focus was always on their target. Typically, we don't look at what could happen, but we look at what did happen. Living by faith is living a life focusing on what God could do.

Living by faith is living a life focusing on what God could do

4. Hang out with people with the same target

It is wise to get around people with the same target. Get away from whiners. Hang out with winners. Find positive people. Take on a project together. This is synergy. It is the philosophy where each builds off each other. Synergy is the concept where 2 people working together accomplish way more than 2 individuals working separately. These 700 men could push each other. They could relate to each other. They could help each other. They could motivate each other. They could celebrate together.

It has been said that left-handed people are the only ones in their right minds. This little joke does apply here. These 700 men were definitely right-minded. They had trained their eye to look forward and make a difference. They were heroes.

Irena Sendler is a hero. During World War II, Irena got permission to work in the Warsaw ghetto as a Plumbing/Sewer specialist. She had an ulterior motive. She knew the plans of the Nazis, so she smuggled infants out in the bottom of her tool box. She had a dog in the back of her truck that she trained to bark at the Nazis when they let her in and out of the camp. This way they couldn't hear a baby making any noise. She would then find foster care for the children. She did keep a list of their names in a jar that she buried in her backyard, hoping she would be able to reunite the families after the war. After rescuing 2,500 infants, she was caught. The Nazis beat her so badly that they broke both her arms and both her legs. She was nominated for the Noble Peace Prize in 2007, but lost to the Global Warming Project of Al Gore. Irena Sendler died in 2008 at the age of 98. She is a hero. Where some people see obstacles, heroes see opportunities to amaze. Irena Sendler knew how to overcome a little while time.

Pictures of Irena Sendler by John Guano

A hero is someone who makes a difference in the world. They are willing to work. They fight through their frustrations. They train their eye on the target. They hang out with people with the same target.

There are two kinds of people: Those who overcome little while times and those who are overcome by little while times.

"Ye are of God, little children, and have overcome them: because greater is He that is in you, than he that is in the world" (1 John 4:4). Greater is He that is in us!

We can't change yesterday, but we can train our eye for the future

Picture by Fabio Venni

"In this world it is not what we take up, but what we give up, that makes us rich."

Henry Ward Beecher

Chapter 5

Bottom Shelf Gospel

You are either coming out of a little while time, in the midst of one or headed for one. They tend to be inevitable. It has been shown that sometimes they are the result of a bad decision we made. However, they can also show up on their own. In

Little while times don't have to be the result of a bad decision

Luke 2, Joseph experienced a little while time that ended up affecting others.

"And it came to pass in those days, that there went out a decree from Caesar Augustus that all the world should be taxed" (verse 1). Caesar of Rome was basically the head of the whole known world. When he needed money, he would institute a tax. As a matter of fact, he would even conquer another area just to receive tax money. He instituted a decree so everyone had to register with the government. The penalty for not paying taxes was not a fine or some jail time; it typically meant death. This was a serious situation. The entire world was going to be taxed.

"(And this taxing was first made when

Cyrenius was governor of Syria.) And all went to be taxed, every one into his own city" (verses 2-3). Luke is writing an accurate historical account so he lets us know the history of when taxes began. He also lets us know that people had to go to their own home town. Everyone went to pay their taxes.

"And Joseph also went up from Galilee, out of the city of Nazareth, into Judaea, unto the city of David, which is called Bethlehem; (because he was of the house and lineage of David) to be taxed with Mary his espoused wife, being great with child" (verses 4-5). Joseph had to go back to his home town of Bethlehem. He had moved up north to Nazareth and now needed to plan for his 90-mile trip. Bethlehem has such beautiful history with Ruth and Boaz getting married and even David playing in the fields. Going home would have some positive memories, but it was a 90-mile walk. Besides that, his wife, Mary, is great with child. This means she was 9 months pregnant. So Joseph is told he has to go back home, his wife is 9 months pregnant and it is a 90-mile walk. This walk will clearly take a full week. It wasn't his idea of a vacation.

"And so it was, that, while they were there, the days were accomplished that she should be delivered" (verse 6). If Joseph didn't feel like he was going through a little while time yet, he would soon. While they were there, Mary is going to give birth. She definitely couldn't travel another week and wait until they got home. It was happening now.

Joseph's attitude had to be tested to the max.

First, the government wants more of his money, his hard earned money. Next he has to travel back home, 90 rough miles. His wife is 9 months pregnant. He has to take her on the trip. Remember, she got pregnant before they were married. This was a punishable offense of death. Joseph may have had to take her to protect her. He couldn't leave her alone. It was definitely a little while time, and it appears it was about to get worse.

"And she brought forth her firstborn son, and wrapped him in swaddling clothes, and laid him in a manger; because there was no room for them in the inn" (verse 7). Joseph knew the town. He knew it only had one inn. The passage didn't say there was no room in the inns. There was one inn and it was full. He couldn't call and make reservations. He just traveled for a week, expecting, that if need be, there to be a place for God's son to be born. It would be a nice place, a comfortable place. But the inn was full,  so he took his 9-month pregnant wife to the place where animals stayed.

Joseph was having a little while time. It involved travel, wife pregnant, taxes, no room in the inn, and now her saying, "It's time." So, the Son of God was born in a manger, a place where animals lived.

There are at least three things we can learn

from Jesus being born in a manger.

1. During little while times, make sure you make godly decisions.

Things that make little while times worse are bad decisions. We need to be careful not to be reactionary. We can't allow these times to send us out of control. Joseph didn't panic; he just kept pressing on.
God wanted Jesus to be born in humility because this King would not be like any other king ever born. This King was born to serve us, to serve the world.

2. During little while times, realize God has a plan.

The church of today doesn't want to believe that God allows us to go through little while times in order to teach us something or prepare us for something. We want to believe that being a Christian means everything will go smoothly, that we won't have problems, and that life will be a bed of roses. The only time something could go wrong is because we sinned. But, as soon as we repent, life will be good again.

However, even in little while times, God has a plan. We need to realize that God has a plan. We need to trust

God because God knows what's best for all of us. Joseph's plan was an inn. That's why he checked out the inn and found it full. God's plan was a manger.

3. Realize your little while time might be going on in your life just so you can help somebody else.

American culture wants to help itself. We are encouraged to watch out for number one. Once we are taken care of, then we can spread our leftovers. But, definitely, we don't want to sacrifice so someone else can benefit. This is contrary to Christian teaching. God designed us to help others. We were called to love and serve one another. You shouldn't live for yourself.

2 Corinthians 1:3-4 is a great reminder, "Blessed be God, even the Father of our Lord Jesus Christ, the Father of mercies, and the God of all comfort; Who comforteth us in all our tribulation, that we may be able to comfort them which are in any trouble, by the comfort wherewith we ourselves are comforted of God." It is possible that God is allowing us to go through a little while time so that we can be taught God's comfort and that we then can use that training to help others. It is the difference between sympathy and empathy.

God always has a plan. Luke 2:8-12 shows us more of the story:

"And there were in the same country

shepherds abiding in the field, keeping watch over their flock by night. And, lo, the angel of the Lord came upon them, and the glory of the Lord shone round about them; and they were sore afraid. And the angel said unto them, Fear not: for, behold, I bring you good tidings of great joy, which shall be to all people. For unto you is born this day in the city of David a Savior, which is Christ the Lord. And this shall be a sign unto you; Ye shall find the babe wrapped in swaddling clothes, lying in a manger."

Shepherds are introduced into the story.

Our view of shepherds may be tainted a little. We see our little boys dress in a robe that is too big, with a funny thing tied on their head, carrying a long stick with a hook. It is cute. It brings a warm fuzzy feeling. We smile and are proud of them. The reality is that shepherds were lowlifes. The Jews viewed it as an unclean profession and even thought being a shepherd would inhibit one's ability to worship. They stunk. They were a horrendous group who were not welcomed into town. People avoided them.

If Jesus was born in a palace, would shepherds be welcomed? Shepherds would not be allowed near the palace. If Jesus was born in the inn, would shepherds be welcomed? Shepherds would not be allowed to see Him. The inn keeper would kick them out so they wouldn't smell up his place and hurt his reputation.

There is only one place where shepherds would be allowed to see Jesus and that place is where animals lived. They found Jesus lying in a manger.

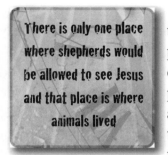

There is only one place where shepherds would be allowed to see Jesus and that place is where animals lived

If you put the Gospel on the top shelf, only the top people will get it. Too many churches and too many pastors view visitors as assets. They wonder what they can expect to get from them, what they have to give. They view certain people as important. They warmly welcome the rich, the elite, and the affluent. They judge by outward appearance and sweep away shepherd-like people. They view a bus ministry as unproductive because it doesn't pay for itself. This was not God's plan.

God's plan from the start was to put the Gospel on the bottom shelf so that the lowliest of the low can reach it so even shepherds have access. It is the relationship based on child-like faith.

Sometimes your little while times are designed by God in preparing to help someone else. This wasn't Joseph's plan, but it was right. The angels told the shepherds: "The Savior has been born. Go see Him. It's okay; He's in a manger."

Luke 1 gives another encouraging thought. When Mary finds out she is carrying God's Son, she is told that her cousin Elizabeth is also pregnant, even 6 months (verse 36). Luke records the greeting John the Baptist gave Jesus before they were even born, as he leaps in the womb (verse 41). Verse 56 shouldn't be missed; "And Mary abode with her about three months, and returned to her own house."

Elizabeth was 6 months pregnant plus the three months Mary visited equals that Mary probably helped in the delivery of John.

Sometimes your little while times are designed by God in preparing to help someone else

God knew Mary would be away from home. She would be basically all alone. So, He prepared her for that special day. God does at times want to use our little while times to help others, but we need to notice that He has prepared us to meet the challenge of that little while time. God has a plan.

Picture by Joel Montes

"Develop success from failures. Discouragement and failure are two of the surest stepping stones to success."
Dale Carnegie

Chapter 6

Be Cool or a Fool

Horatio Spafford is a hero. Spafford was a successful lawyer who faced several traumatic events. His four-year-old son died. The Great Chicago Fire ruined him financially. Finally, when moving to Europe, he sent his family ahead of him as he finished some business. His four daughters were on a different ship than his wife. Their ship was struck by a sailing ship, causing it to sink. All four girls were killed. Spafford left to be reunited with his grieving wife. The captain let Spafford know when they passed the area where his daughters drowned. At that moment, he was inspired to write these words:

When peace, like a river, attendeth my way,
When sorrows like sea billows roll;
Whatever my lot, Thou hast taught me to say,
It is well, it is well, with my soul.

Refrain:
It is well, with my soul,
It is well, with my soul,

It is well, it is well, with my soul.

Though Satan should buffet, though trials should come,
Let this blest assurance control,
That Christ has regarded my helpless estate,
And hath shed His own blood for my soul.

Horatio Spafford experienced some of the worst tricks life can throw at us. In this little while time, he acknowledged that God was in control, and it brought peace. Once the daughters died, his wife's telegram to him said, "Saved alone..." Not much else is written about her response. It is safe to say that she felt robbed and cheated by life.

In Nehemiah chapter 5, Nehemiah has to respond to some angry women. Nehemiah was called to rebuild the walls and gates of Jerusalem. He left his comfortable lifestyle to go back home and take on a major challenge for God. He found out a basic principle of life: anytime you plan on doing something for God, the enemy will show up. External opposition is expected, but there is often internal opposition, too. We tend to prepare for the outside opposition, but our friends and family catch us off guard when they turn on us.

Nehemiah's men were building the walls with a sword in one hand and a trowel in the other. They were ready for the enemy to attack at any time. However, verse 1 brings an internal battle, "And there was a great cry of the people and of their wives against their brethren the Jews." The women were complaining. People often tease, "If momma ain't happy, ain't nobody happy." We then laugh as we realize the truth of the statement. Proverbs 21:9 says, "It is better to dwell in a corner of the housetop, than with a brawling woman in a wide house." This statement is so powerful it is repeated in Proverbs 25:24. An upset woman isn't typically good at hiding her feelings. Nehemiah finds out the women are mad.

We men need to acknowledge that normally when a lady is mad, she has a good reason. Men tend to be conquerors, while women are the queens of the castle. Men are off looking for a challenge, while women are  home with too many responsibilities and not enough help. She probably has a good reason for not being happy. Nehemiah finds this to be true.

The women are complaining because there is not enough food, "For there were those that said, We, our sons, and our daughters, are many; therefore we take up corn for them, that we may eat, and live" (verse 2). Women are willing to put up with a lot, but when the children are hungry, it is time for action. The women are right in complaining, as there isn't enough food. But, it gets worse.

The women are complaining because they have had to mortgage their property, "Some also there were that said, We have mortgaged our lands, vineyards, and houses, that we might buy corn, because of the dearth" (verse 3). Their men are away, there is no food or grain, the children are hungry, and now they have to mortgage their property for food. But, it gets worse.

The women are complaining because they have to borrow money to pay their taxes. "There were also those that said, We have borrowed money for the king's tribute, and that upon our lands and vineyards" (verse 4). The women complained that they had to pay usury, even 12%. The women complained and were right. But, it gets worse.

The women are complaining because their children are being sold into slavery, "Yet now our flesh is as the flesh of our brethren, our children as their children: and, lo, we bring into bondage our sons and our daughters to be servants, and some of our daughters are brought unto bondage already; neither is it in our power to redeem them; for other men have our lands and vineyards" (verse 5). While the men are away, people are taking advantage of the women. There is no food, they have mortgaged their property, they have taxes and usury, and now their children are being sold into slavery. The women are mad and that might be an understatement.

Nehemiah becomes angry, "And I was very angry when I heard their cry and these words" (verse 6). Nehemiah listened, and what he heard got him mad. He was angry. Anger can be the battleground for most men. It also affects women. Things are said that can't be unsaid. Things are done that can't be undone. Kids hear things they shouldn't hear. Proverbs 14:17 says, "He that is soon angry dealeth foolishly." We need to learn to control anger. It needs tight reigns.

Anger by itself is not sin. Ephesians 4:26 says, "Be ye angry, and sin not: let not the sun go down upon your wrath." There are some things that should make us angry. There are things that make us mad and that we act upon. Proverbs 22:15 says, "Foolishness is bound in the heart of a child." Children are vulnerable and easily misguided. We need to be angry when they are hurt or directed wrongly. When a first-grader comes home saying that a family can be a dad and a dad or a mom and a mom, we should be angry. This is not being homophobic; it is sinophobic. Yes, we are to love people and hate sin. We should be angry when wrong is made to be right. Sin should make us angry.

Anger is not the problem - our reaction is. Nehemiah sets a great example in verse 7, "Then I consulted with myself." Nehemiah was angry, so he consulted himself. This sounds funny. It has been said, "It is okay to talk to yourself, just don't answer." Nehemiah is talking to himself. Nehemiah heard  the women, and he was mad. He didn't want to say something that he couldn't undo. He wasn't going to react until he consulted himself. A key to making sure little while times don't create new little while times is to consult ourselves as soon as we get angry. Before we respond, we need to seek counsel from ourselves. It is better to remain cool than to immediately respond out of anger and be a fool.

When little while times come, we need to remember that God is in control and has a bigger plan. Instead of immediately acting out of control, we consult ourselves and say, "It is well with my soul."

Picture by Manish Bansal

"Success is simple. Do what's right, the right way, at the right time."

Arnold H. Glasow

Chapter 7

String on My Finger

Have you ever lost your car? Have you ever been shopping and, when you came out on to the parking lot, you couldn't remember where you parked? Engineers knew we would forget, so they added a button to help us find our car. The panic button is for emergencies and maybe a silly prank, but it is most often used to help us remember where we parked our car. A simple principle can be developed from this: If you don't remember where you have been, it won't be likely you will get to where you need to go.

Having a good memory can be helpful. The word "remember" is used 144 times in the Bible. God repeats Himself over one hundred times telling us to remember something. Typically, when someone repeats something, it is important. Our culture is so driven that most messages focus on passages like Philippians 3:14: "I press toward the mark for the prize of the high calling of God in Christ Jesus." It is good to press forward, but God reminds us to remember and, "if He told us once, He told us a hundred times" or more precisely, 144!

In Joshua chapter 4, the Lord tells Joshua to set up a memorial. Moses has died, and Joshua is the new leader. The people have wandered for 40 years, and now it is time to enter the Promised Land. In order to enter the Promised Land, they must cross the Jordan River. In chapter 3, we are told that, although it was the rainy season and the water was up to the banks, the people crossed on dry land. Once they cross, the Lord tells Joshua to choose 12 men (Joshua 4:2). Each man is to take a stone from the river bed and carry it to the other side of the Jordan River. It wasn't just a stone or a pebble; the Lord wanted something more substantial. The men picked up larger rocks and put them on their shoulders as they crossed over (verse 5). The 12 stones were put in a pile as a sign for future generations: "That this may be a sign among you, that when your children ask their fathers in time to come, saying, What mean ye by these stones" (verse 6)? The Lord is setting up the stones so that people will wonder why. He then gives the answer in verse 7: "Then ye shall answer them, That the waters of Jordan were cut off before the ark of the covenant of the LORD; when it passed over Jordan, the waters of Jordan were cut off: and these stones shall be for a memorial unto the children of Israel for ever." These stones were set as a memorial. The pile was created to remind future generations of the past.

It was a Memorial unto the children of Israel forever

You have to know where you came from to

know where you are going. We can't forget where we have been, or we might not be able to get where we need to go. The stones were set as a reminder of where they had been. They were wandering and out of God's will. Yet, God did not forget His promise and brought them into a new stage of life. God has great plans for the life of His people. There are at least 3 reasons why we need to remember where we have been if we are going to get where we need to go. We may be stalled in our little while time because we haven't learned or gathered enough from the past.

1. If you don't remember where you have been, you will forget the people in your life who have done amazing things for you.

We all have had amazing people in our life. We need to remember the past, so we don't forget what they have done for us. We need to honor and thank the people who have influenced our life. The last

We need to honor and thank the people who have influenced our life

Monday in May has been set aside as Memorial Day. It is a day to remember those in the military. It is those whom we may never have met, but who have drastically impacted our life and our freedom.

There are other people from our past that deserve recognition. From the moment we were born, our mothers have sacrificed a lot for us. This is not about finding people who were perfect in our life. Only Jesus was perfect. This is about finding people who, in certain ways, had a positive impact on us. Our parents are our starting point. It may be a teacher, coach, neighbor, youth pastor, friend or employer who really helped us move in the right direction. We need to stop, remember them and, if possible, thank them. This is so important, that maybe you should set down this book and call, text, email, write a letter, or even visit them and say thank you. Let them know that you remember them.

2. We need to remember where we came from, so we can remember what we were.

We need to remember that all of us were a mess before we came to know Jesus Christ as Savior. Unfortunately, Christians can act as if they deserved to be saved or as if they did something special  to be honored in such a way. Most of us have heard and possibly even memorized Ephesians 2:8-9: "For by grace are ye saved through faith; and that not of yourselves: it is the gift of God- Not of works, lest any man should boast." Cognitively, we know our salvation was a gift and not by our works, yet we act as better than those who are searching. We need to acknowledge Romans 3:10: "As it is written,

There is none righteous, no, not one." We need to remember our past. We need to remember what we were before without Jesus.

A common theme taught among the church growth leaders is to be careful with whom you spend time. The lesson is that to succeed as a Pastor you need to only spend time with people of influence - important people. Pastors are busy, so they shouldn't invest their time where it won't produce. This is sad and even sin. Everyone is important to God! The most famous verse in the Bible is a good reminder: "For God so loved the world, that he gave his only begotten Son, that whosoever believeth in him should not perish, but have everlasting life" (John 3:16). God loved the world. He loved and loves us. He loved so much that He gave the ultimate gift, His Son.

We need to remember what we were before Jesus came into our life. We are now blessed. Our salvation is not the only time God moves around and for us.

3. We need to remember where we are from so we don't forget God is working in our lives.

God has been working in our lives. We need to remember what He has already done. Joshua chapter 4 was about setting up a memorial to remind future generations what God had done at the Jordan River. Joshua chapter 3 tells the story.

"And it shall come to pass, as soon as the

soles of the feet of the priests that bear the ark of the
LORD, the LORD of all the earth, shall rest in the
waters of Jordan, that the waters of Jordan shall be
cut off from the waters that come down from above;
and they shall stand upon an heap" (verse 13). It is
beautiful how the Lord tests their trust. The Lord
tells them they are going to cross over the Jordan.
But, before He divides the water, He has the priests
step forward into the water.

In verse 15, a factor is given: "And as they
that bare the ark were come unto Jordan, and the
feet of the priests that bare the ark were dipped in
the brim of the water, (for Jordan overfloweth all its
banks all the time of harvest,)." The factor is that
it is the rainy season. This is not a time when the
water level is low and one could try to gently step
through the river. No, the passage says that the banks
overflow with water. The rainy season follows a dry
time when the ground gets baked and becomes very
hard. The rain from the mountains flows down to the
low areas where the Jordan River comes through.
The water level was high.

As soon as the feet of the priests hit the water,
the water backed up: "That the waters which came
down from above stood and rose up upon an heap
very far from the city Adam, that is beside Zaretan;
and those that came down toward the sea of the
plain, even the salt sea, failed, and were cut off: and
the people passed over right against Jericho" (verse
16). It states that the people crossed over in the area
of Jericho, but that the water backed up to the area

of Zaretan. The stones would remind the future generations what this meant. The passage doesn't need to give the distance, since it states the cities. All Israelites would know the distance, but we might miss it. It was about 20 miles. The Lord backed up the river about 20 miles. Verse 17 tells us that they then passed over on dry ground. This was something worth remembering and something that needed to be passed on to others.

We need to remember God is working upstream for us. We are encouraged to pray. So, we pray regularly and God answers. However, we often go back to just asking, begging and pleading without ever acknowledging what God has done in  the past. Our prayer journal should have a section detailing the answers to prayer. Maybe a larger section of our prayer time should be that of thanking God specifically for the great things He has done for us, in us, and through us. Maybe we should set up our own memorial to remind us of a specific miracle. The memorial doesn't have to be a pile of rocks; it might be the planting of a tree or a framed verse with explanation framed on the wall. We need to remember what God has done.

Often, during a little while time, we just want to press the fast-forward button on our personal remote. Although this can be tempting, we may miss seeing God work directly in our life. During these tough times, we need to remember how He has been faithful in the past. This will give us the confidence to face the next day.

Picture by John Haslam

"Success is to be measured not so much by the position that one has reached in life as by the obstacles which he has overcome."

Booker T. Washington

Chapter 8

Grapes – Giants – Grasshoppers

A family goes out for dinner one night. It is not a common occurrence for them; it is a special event. The family loads up the minivan and heads for the restaurant. The mom, dad and kids all sit down in the restaurant and place their orders. When the food arrives, dad asks the 6-year-old son to pray. The boy prays, "Dear Jesus, Thank you for my family and for our food, and I pray that you would help dad buy ice cream when we get done with our meal. Amen."

Most people in the restaurant chuckled. One older lady got up and walked over to the table. She folded her arms. While shaking a pointed finger at the boy, she said, "Little boy, that was a disrespectful little prayer. You don't even know how to pray." She continued as if giving a speech to everyone in earshot: "That is the problem with kids today – they don't respect God and ask for things like ice cream." Focusing back on the boy, she concluded, "God doesn't care about your ice cream and you shouldn't pray things like that." She went back to her seat and sat down.

The whole restaurant was still with shock.

The little boy was trying not to cry when an older man, who had been sitting by himself in the corner, got up and came over to him. The man knelt down on a knee and whispered, "I thought your prayer was terrific. In fact, I have heard that ice cream is good for the soul." He stood up, patted the boy on the head, walked over to his seat and signaled for the waitress. As the restaurant atmosphere returned to its normal shuffle, the man told the waitress that when the family finishes eating, he wanted her to bring ice cream sundaes for the entire family and that he would pay for it.

Not too long later, the waitress came out with a tray of big ice cream sundaes. The boy's eyes lit up, as did the rest of the family. She set one sundae if front of each family member. The little boy looked at his and a huge smile crossed his face. His eyes and words expressed appreciation to his father, who was speechless as he was caught off guard.

The little boy grabbed his spoon, started for a big scoop, shook his head and set the spoon down. Again, he started to take a spoon full, but shook his head and set his spoon down. Finally, he just said, "Okay" and stood up. He picked up his ice cream, walked across the room over to where the older lady sat, placed it in front of her and said, "Ma'am, I want you to have my ice cream sundae. I hear it is good for the soul." As he walked away, he chimed, "And by the way, my soul is already good."

The story is a cute reminder that we need to look for blessings. In Numbers 13, the nation of Israel has come to the edge of the border of the Promised Land. It is time for them to enter God's blessing. They had left the bondage of the Egyptians, crossed the Red Sea in one of the all time greatest miracles, and they were now getting ready to walk into the promises of God.

Moses chooses 12 men. He calls them spies. He wants them to go check out the land. He wants to find out what he is up against. They go over there for 40 days checking out the Promised Land. They find out that their enemies are great. Some of the enemies are in the mountains, while others reside by the coast. On top of that, they have great walled cities. However, the worse news was that the children of Anak were there. The children of Anak were giants. They were massive men. They were huge and scared the Israelites. Numbers 13:25-26 reports, "At the end of forty days they returned from spying out the land. And they came to Moses and Aaron and to all the congregation of the people of Israel in the wilderness of Paran, at Kadesh. They brought back word to them and to all the congregation, and showed them the fruit of the land."

When the 12 spies brought back their findings, they start off positive: "And they told him, "We came to the land to which you sent us. It flows with milk and honey, and this is its fruit" (verse 27). They show the fruit and report that God

God's promises are real

has brought them to a special land. The land is milk and honey. God's promises are real. They even bring back grapes as a picture of God's promises.

Even though the land is sweet, the spies bring a sour aspect to it: "However, the people who dwell in the land are strong, and the cities are fortified and very large. And besides, we saw the descendants of Anak there. The Amalekites dwell in the land of the Negeb. The Hittites, the Jebusites, and the Amorites dwell in the hill country. And the Canaanites dwell by the sea, and along the Jordan" (verses 28-29).

Numbers 13:30-33 shows the split in perspective: "But Caleb quieted the people before Moses and said, 'Let us go up at once and occupy it, for we are well able to overcome it.' Then the men who had gone up with him said, "We are not able to go up against the people, for they are stronger than we are.' So they brought to the people of Israel a bad report of the land that they had spied out, saying, 'The land, through which we have gone to spy it out, is a land that devours its inhabitants, and all the people that we saw in it are of great height. And there we saw the Nephilim (the sons of Anak, who come from the Nephilim), and we seemed to ourselves like grasshoppers, and so we seemed to them.'"

Caleb, one of the spies, speaks up saying that the land is their land. He voices his vote that they need to go take the land God has given them. He wants to move forward. However, 10 of the spies basically say that they would rather go back to Egypt and be in bondage. They are scared. They fear the giants. They say that they are just grasshoppers in comparison to these giants.

There are 3 key words from this section. The words even flow with some alliteration: Grapes, Giants, and Grasshoppers.

1. Grapes represent the blessings of God.

God is in the blessing business. God wants to bless His people. Adam and Eve started with many blessings. They were put in a place of many blessings. Fathers enjoy seeing their children smile and giggle. Likewise, God takes joy in blessing His children. Malachi 3:10 clearly displays this concept: "Bring the full tithe into the storehouse, that there may be food in my house. And thereby put me to

the test, says the Lord of hosts, if I will not open the windows of heaven for you and pour down for you a blessing until there is no more need." God asks us to test Him. We are to step out in obedience and see His response.

God says He is going to pour out the blessings. It doesn't say He will hand us a blessing; He will pour blessings. Do you remember the trick-n-treat adventure? It was fun to go to a house and receive a piece of candy. It was better when some generous adult gave us a handful of candy. It was over-the-top when someone said we were their last guest and they poured the rest of the bowl into our bag. God isn't talking about handing us a blessing. He is talking about pouring a blessing. He wants to open the windows of Heaven and pour out His blessings. Instead of a blessing, He is pouring out a 55-gallon blessing, or dump truck's worth, or even a tandem hauler full of blessing.

The grapes that were brought back were delicious. They were a sign that the land was milk and honey. They represented God's blessings.

Acts chapter 3 records when Peter and John are traveling and Peter heals the crippled beggar. This miracle leads to a discussion where Peter reminds the people that Jesus came to bless them. Acts 3:24-26 says, "And all the prophets who have spoken, from Samuel and those who came after him, also proclaimed these days. You are the sons of the prophets and of the covenant that God made with your fathers, saying to Abraham, 'And in your offspring shall all the families of the earth be blessed.' God, having raised up his servant, sent him to you first, to bless you by turning every one of you from your wickedness." Twice in these verses he refers to the word bless. Jesus came to bless. God wants to bless. We need to be open and receptive to His blessings.

Paul speaks in Galatians that the sons of Abraham didn't want the blessings, so He gave it to the Gentiles. Galatians 3:9 says, "So then, those who are of faith are blessed along with Abraham, the man of faith." The children of Israel have always been God's chosen people, but now He has included Gentiles. They have been grafted in. God's blessings are open to all people.

Warning: The world wants to believe that God is going to bless you no matter how you live. This isn't true.

Blessings hinge on obedience.

The people of Israel couldn't get the blessings of the Promised Land until they went in. They needed to take the step of obedience. They wandered 40 years being disciplined by God because they weren't obedient. Blessings come with obedience. "Do not be deceived: God is not mocked, for whatever one sows, that will he also reap" (Galatians 6:7). You will reap what you sow.

Evaluate your little while time. Are you obedient to God? Remember, blessings come with obedience. Sometimes we bring little while times on ourselves by not being obedient to God and His principles.

If my marriage is struggling, I need to ask, "Am I obedient to God in my actions and reactions with my spouse?"

If my children are my source of feeling cursed, I need to ask, "Am I raising my children to be obedient to God?"

If I am not experiencing a blessed life, I need to ask, "Am I living a life that is characterized by obedience to God and His Word?

The grapes represented the blessings of God. These blessings could only be received through obedience.

2. Giants represent obstacles.

If you are going to do anything for God, then you will face obstacles. Satan is not just going to sit back without a fight. Sometimes you have to roll up your sleeves and battle. If everything is going smoothly, it could be a sign that you are on the wrong road. The grapes often come after the giants are dealt with. Blessings come after obedience. Obedience means dealing with giants. The enemy doesn't want you to experience the blessings of God.

All the Israelites wanted the blessing. This was not the problem.

All the Israelites were used to experiencing obstacles. This was not the problem.

The problem was that they viewed them-selves as grasshoppers.

3. Grasshoppers represent the absence of leadership.

"And there we saw the Nephilim (the sons of Anak, who come from the Nephilim), and we seemed to ourselves like grasshoppers, and so we seemed to them" (Numbers 13:33). They viewed themselves as grasshoppers. This is the problem.

Proverbs 30:27 says, "The locusts have no king, yet all of them march in rank." In the Hebrew, the words locust and grasshopper are used interchangeably. They meant the same thing. They were synonymous.

The locust has no king. The grasshopper has no king. The 10 spies viewed themselves as grasshoppers. They viewed themselves as one who has no king. This is the problem.

We have a king. We don't just have a king, but the King of Kings. Our King is the One who cut the Grand Canyon. He is the One who painted the sky blue. He hung the stars. He is the King of the universe. He is the King of Kings.

You are not a grasshopper. The Israelites did not know who they were. They had no king. Or better said, they forgot they had a king. Instead of seeing their King, they saw the giants.

There is no obstacle you will face that is too big for your King.

You have to realize who you are. If you are a child of God, and if you have experienced the redemptive work of Jesus Christ, then you are not a grasshopper. A grasshopper doesn't have a king. You have a King.

My King has never faced an obstacle too big for Him.

The Israelites had a problem. It wasn't about wanting a blessing. It wasn't about obstacles. It was about identity. They forgot they had a King.

Adoption is a beautiful option to adding to you family. One of the struggles that can come with adoption is identity. Some adoptive children don't know who their dad is or if they have one. They don't initially realize that they now have a father who is their dad. This can be true of Christians.

Those of us who have experienced salvation in Jesus Christ are now adopted by God. If adopted by God, then we are a child of the King.

Do you struggle with who you are? Remind yourself that you are not a grasshopper because you have a King.

Discover who you are so the obstacles don't overcome you.

I have a King, the King, the King of Kings.

By the way, in history some people were used and abused by their king. Our King loved and loves us so much that He feels we are worth dying for.

Maybe the little boy who prayed for ice cream understood he was a child of the King. During your little while time, pray for God's blessings and remember who you are.

Picture by Sean MacEntee

"Success is the progressive realization of
predetermined, worthwhile, personal goals."
Paul J. Meyer

Chapter 9

Dancing with God

Do you remember Junior High dances? Typically, boys were on one side of the gym while girls stood on the other side. Everyone was nervous to take the first step. Probably if someone had started a game of Red Rover, it would have helped. Most guys just hung out with their friends and never approached the dance floor. The same floor that they just ran up and down while diving for a basketball, was now untouchable as covered in lava. They chose to sit this one out.

In life, do you tend to sit it out or dance? I understand personalities. Introverts tend to sit it out when life experiences come their way. They miss opportunities that maybe they were meant to experience. Extroverts (Sanguine, High "I's", Otters) jump into the dance circle and experience life to the fullest. Maybe it is sometimes more about courage than personality.

With God, is your relationship one that you would say you are sitting this one out or are you dancing? This has nothing to do with personality and everything to do with perspective and passion. God wants to dance with us.

Philippians 1:21 is one of Paul's most quoted

verses: "and to die is gain." It is a "go-to" verse in ministry. I serve now knowing that my death brings reward. It is interesting that although the verse is only 12 words long, people and even pastors tend to only focus on the last 4 words. The verse unfortunately becomes known as a verse focusing on death. Paul was not focusing on death, but life. He wasn't focusing on dancing in Heaven, but in serving God with his life daily. He was dancing with God now.

Paul was not teaching people how to die, but how to live. His emphasis was on life. The previous verse says, "As it is my eager expectation and hope that I will not be at all ashamed, but that with full courage now as always Christ will be honored in my body, whether by life or by death" (Philippians 1:20). His focus is on life so he won't be ashamed in death. His thoughts are to live with no regrets.

Paul's emphasis is to live for Christ. Everyone lives for something. For some people, their job becomes their identity. They live for their job. For others it may be a sport. They are consumed with a team or activity. There are even shirts that read, "Life is golf" or "Life is fishing." Everyone

lives for something. There are 3 thoughts that should be considered when we evaluate what we live for.

1. Living for Christ never ends.

Realize that whatever you choose to live for, when it ends, your life ends. You might not physically die, but you stop existing. If my life is my motorcycle, then when I can't drive anymore, my life ends. It is sad, but this can be true of relationships. Moms who live for their children can feel extremely lost when the nest is empty.

Living for Christ is different. When I die, then there is gain. It even gets better. No other option gives this fulfillment and reward. The topic remains life with a little extra topping.

What do you live for?

2. Living for Christ opens the windows of Heaven.

When you live for Christ, you not only live for something that doesn't end, you are living for something that opens the windows for the unexplainable. This is a different perspective. Some people are satisfied with just the logical. Everything needs to make sense, predictable. However, living for Christ doesn't always seem to make sense. There are those times that we call God-incidences. They are not coincidences. They are much more purposeful. Their timing is divine. They are unexplainable, supernatural, and nonsensical. It is in these times that we know God is in the house.

To live for Christ gives purpose and meaning. It is something that can affect every day. Matthew 25:40 reminds us to treat everyone as created in the image of God: "And the King will answer them, 'Truly, I say to you, as you did it to one of the least of these my  brothers, you did it to me.'" When we reach out to those who are hurting, we, in essence, are reaching out to Christ. We are living for Christ. Our job is to live for God. When this happens, unbelievable things will happen that end up strengthening our faith. It is ironic that the unbelievable events strengthen faith.

There is great benefit in living for Christ. Not only do we live for something that never ends, and that opens the windows of Heaven, but there is at least one more benefit.

3. Living for Christ allows one to rise above disappointments.

This book talks a lot about disappointments. It is those little while times that can drag us down. However, living for Christ seems to allow us to rise above all the disappointments of life. Life will hurt. If you are not living for Christ, the hurts will kick the life right out of you.

Paul's context is darkened by potential

disappointment when he concludes, "For to me to live is Christ, and to die is gain." Philippians 1:15-18 says,

"Some indeed preach Christ from envy and rivalry, but others from good will. The latter do it out of love, knowing that I am put here for the defense of the gospel. The former proclaim Christ out of selfish ambition, not sincerely but thinking to afflict me in my imprisonment. What then? Only that in

every way, whether in pretense or in truth, Christ is proclaimed, and in that I rejoice."

It has been brought to Paul's attention that some people were preaching about Jesus Christ just so Paul would be afflicted. Not only is he in prison for the Lord, but he is being afflicted while in prison because of others preaching. In this, he does not complain. He rejoices that Jesus is proclaimed. Paul knew how to dance with shackles on. He chose to dance in prison with the Lord. He lived for Christ. His focus was on life.

When you live for Christ, it gives you the ability to rise above all disappointment. Living for Christ can often be measured on how you respond to difficulties. Remember difficulties can be from God to help us live for Christ.

Years ago, Pastor Jim and his wife were at a diner with 3 of their sons. The waitress was walking by when she accidentally dumped a soda on his head. It went all over him. His boys busted out laughing. He smiled and assured her all was okay as he excused himself to the restroom to wash up. The waitress was obviously panicked, but Pastor Jim was calm. They enjoyed the meal and Pastor's wife even left a nice tip (feel free to read into that one if you want).

That Sunday the waitress came to his church. The next week she came forward to get saved. Later, she was asked what brought her to the church. She explained how she dumped a pop on a man. He was gracious about it. She found out he was a pastor. She wanted to find out how someone could act like that, so she came to his church.

No one gets it right all the time, but Pastor Jim scored this time. It was obvious he was living for Christ and not himself. The story goes on. Later, Pastor Jim officiated her wedding with her husband. Her husband now leads worship at one of the church campuses that Pastor Jim helped launch. Recently, she was able to get Pastor Jim a speaking engagement at a secular university which is now leading to opportunities in some public high schools. He isn't able to share Christ at the event, but many of the students start following him on Twitter or come to an evening service at a local church.

Remember, she came to church because when she heard he was a pastor, she wanted to find out what it was all about that could allow someone to respond the way he did. When you live for Christ, it gives you the ability to rise above all disappointments.

Philippians 1 has another verse that is a beautiful promise: "And I am sure of this, that he who began a good work in you will bring it to completion at the day of Jesus Christ" (verse 6). When we live for Christ, we find out that He is the completer of our life. Jesus is working in us, and He isn't done. He still has big plans.

We all live for something. The only choice that never ends, that opens the windows of Heaven, and that allows us to rise above our little while times, is living for Christ.

James 4:8 says, "Draw near to God, and he will draw near to you." You don't need to cross the gym floor. Just draw near to God, and let Him lead the dance.

Picture by Pete Coleman

"Success isn't a result of spontaneous combustion. You must set yourself on fire."
                                        Arnold H. Glasow

Chapter 10

Water Boy?

Larry Walters wanted to fly. So, in 1982, he bought a lawn chair from Sears and 45 weather balloons from a surplus store. He attached the balloons to the chair, packed some sandwiches, a pellet gun and a six-pack of beer (that may explain his thought patterns). His friends cut him loose. He thought he would fly about 30 feet over his Los Angeles neighbors' houses as he waved and greeted them. However, he didn't just soar to 30 feet, or 100 feet, or 1,000 feet, but over 10,000 feet. Pilots flying nearby were quoted as saying, "You are never going to believe it." Larry became nervous and thought he should shoot out a couple of balloons. He descended quickly and wasn't totally in control as he got caught in some power lines. The local authorities rescued him and then cuffed him, assuming he had broken some aviation law. When asked, "Why would you do such a stupid thing?" Larry responded, "Man can't just sit there."

Larry has a good point. We were not created by God to just sit there. There is a disease creeping into Christianity and the church that is killing it. People are just sitting. People are missing out on their lives and Christianity by just sitting there. .

There are studies made of what the most dangerous items are in the common household. Two to three million people get hurt using knives in the kitchen every year in America. About 900,000  people get injured from their power tools in the garage. The curtains hurt some people, while pillows hurt a few thousand. However, the most dangerous item in the common household is probably the easy chair. Unfortunately, too many people believe that the easy chair with the TV remote control is the ideal picture of what life was meant to be. We just sit there.

A few years ago, some scientists put an amoeba in what they called a perfect environment. They evaluated what the perfect temperature with ample food supply would yield. There were no pressures, difficulties, adversity or problems. When placed there, the amoeba died. It is not good even for an amoeba to just sit there.

People think they don't want difficulties. They think life would be better if they didn't have to face problems or adversity. There is a belief that if they are going through a struggle, something must be wrong. Therefore, people tend to put on a mask. They play religion. They pretend all is well.

The reality is that we all face adversity. It may be health, finances or family. It may be physical, emotional, or spiritual. But we all will have struggles. We are either in a little while time, just coming out of one, or about to enter one. And it can be a mixture of those three. We all have struggles. The key is how we view them. There are at least 3 myths about adversity. Before we expose the three myths, it is valuable to set the stage found in Mark 14:12-16:

And on the first day of Unleavened Bread, when they sacrificed the Passover lamb, his disciples said to him, "Where will you have us go and prepare for you to eat the Passover?" And he sent two of his disciples and said to them, "Go into the city, and a man carrying a jar of water will meet you. Follow him, and wherever he enters, say to the master of the house, 'The Teacher says, Where is my guest room, where I may eat the Passover with my disciples?' And he will show you a large upper room furnished and ready; there prepare for us." And the disciples set out and went to the city and found it just as he had told them, and they prepared the Passover.

Jesus is getting ready to be sold for 30 pieces of silver. He is about to face the cross. It is just hours away. He will be beaten and humiliated. He will die shortly and even go to the grave. However, the best part is that He will rise again (and He did).

It is with this backdrop that He meets with His disciples. One of them asks a natural question, "Where are we going to celebrate the Passover?" Knowing the events surrounding these days, we might not think this is an important question, but to a Jew it is crucial. Passover was the High Holy Day for Jews, and Jesus and His disciples were Jews. This was the day they remember being set free. It was when the angel of the Lord killed the firstborn of every Egyptian family, but would "pass over" the Israelite homes if they put the blood of the lamb on their doorpost. Even non-orthodox Jews enjoyed the meal, tradition, family and friends. This feast was special.

Jesus tells two of the disciples to go into town where they will meet a man who is carrying water. This can sound strange. Jerusalem was jammed pack. Everyone was coming to Jerusalem - it is the holy city. The gates were filled, and the streets  were crowded. People were everywhere. Jesus said they needed to find the man carrying the water. That sounds too vague. They didn't have running water and indoor plumbing, so everyone had to carry water. This sounds quite random to say, "Find a man carrying water." However, Jewish tradition and custom lets us know that men never carried water. It was women's work. It would be a disgrace for a man to carry water. He would be humiliated. Remember the woman at the well (John 4) came after the other women had drawn water. Isaac meets his wife as she is drawing water (Genesis 24). Real men didn't draw water.

There were three groups of Jewish men in the

first century: Pharisees, Sadducees and Essenes. The Pharisees and Sadducees are often following Jesus to try and trick him. They were separate from each other in regards to beliefs like the resurrection. The Pharisees were "fair you see" as they believed in a resurrection, while the Sadducees were "sad you see" as they didn't. The area of commonality was that they liked the prestige, power and finances of their position, and they both felt Jesus was a threat to it. The Pharisees and Sadducees would never be caught carrying water. The Essenes were a different group.

Josephus, the early Jewish historian, records that the Essenes were a group of men near Qumran. They had a high regard for Scripture and are the scribes of the Dead Sea Scrolls. John the Baptist was an Essenes. Essenes never married. They felt women would be a distraction from their mission of following the Word.

Jesus tells the two disciples to find a man carrying water and follow him. They didn't need to talk with him, just follow him. He will take them to the room, the upper room. The adversity in the life of the disciples was where to celebrate the Passover. This was important. It was as important as anything else to a Jew. This was truly an adversity for them. Jesus says, "Follow the man with the water."

"Follow the man with water" leads to an interesting study. Ephesians 5:25-27 speaks of water as symbolizing the Word of God: "Husbands, love your wives, as Christ loved the church and gave himself up for her, that he might sanctify her, having cleansed her by the washing of water with the word, so that he might present the church to himself in splendor, without spot or wrinkle or any such thing, that she might be holy and without blemish." Paul speaks of washing of water by the use of the Word. "Follow the man with water" is a great reminder for us that when we are in the midst of adversity, the solution is to follow the man who is carrying the Word of God. God's Word can encourage and correct us in times of need. We don't know the name of the man carrying the water. He was not to be the

 emphasis. The focal point was to be the water, the Word of God. Focus on the Word.

Like the amoeba, we were meant to experience adversity. Everyone will have to deal with it. As you, or those near you, face adversity, please don't fall into the trap of these 3 myths.

Myth #1: Adversity is bad for us.

Our bodies are wired to avoid pain. It is natural to assume that adversity is bad for us. Our society emphasizes the easy road. All too often we hear, "If it feels good, do it." We don't want adversity. We want easy street.

Recently, Pastor Jim and his younger brother,

who is also a pastor, were analyzing where they get their passion. Pastor Jim's brother made a profound discovery that their pain produced their passion. They had been raised by a unbelieving father and then by a believing father. They were raised in a home that did not recognize God, and then in a home that was godly. They knew what it was like to not have God in their life, and what it was like to have God in their life. They believe that is what drives them. They want everyone they come in contact with to experience God. Adversity in childhood gave birth to passion for God. We need to thank God for the things that made us what we are. Pain can be good in producing passion for God.

God tells Joshua that as he becomes the new leader, he will need two things. The two items are not a easy chair and a remote control. The two items are to be strong and courageous. Joshua 1:6-9 says,

Be strong and courageous, for you shall cause this people to inherit the land that I swore to their fathers to give them. Only be strong and very courageous, being careful to do according to all the law that Moses my servant commanded you. Do not turn from it to the right hand or to the left, that you may have good success wherever you go. This Book of the Law shall not depart from your mouth, but you shall meditate on it day and night, so that you may be careful to do according to all that is written in it. For then you will make your way prosperous, and then you will have good success. Have I not commanded you? Be strong and courageous. Do not be frightened, and do not be dismayed, for the Lord your God is with you wherever you go."

God doesn't tell Joshua that He will take his problems away. He doesn't tell him to avoid his problems. He says to be strong and courageous. Why does God tell Joshua to be strong and courageous? God knows adversity will come. God lets Joshua know that he will have adversity and that it is okay. God tells him to stay focused on the path, keep to the Word, and God Himself will be with him. It reminds us to roll up our sleeves, grit our teeth and press on so we can see what God is going to do. Adversity allows us to see God do something incredible. The bigger the problem, the bigger the response. God is awesome.

Joseph had a proper response to adversity. In Genesis 50, when his father dies and his brothers think he will take revenge on them, he says, "Do not fear, for am I in the place of God? As for you, you meant evil  against me, but God meant it for good, to bring it about that many people should be kept alive, as they are today" (verses 19-20). Joseph asks a rhetorical question, "Am I in the place of God?" He was second in charge. He was the man. He doesn't blame his childhood or pout about slavery and prison. He realized God used adversity to make him the man he was. God also used that man to save a nation. People

The bigger the problem, the bigger the response

may cause adversity in our lives. They may mean to hurt us, but God can use it for good. God wins.

The half-brother of Jesus understood adversity and how one should perceive it, "Count it all joy, my brothers, when you meet trials of various kinds, for you know that the testing of your faith produces steadfastness. And let steadfastness have its full effect, that you may be perfect and complete, lacking in nothing" (James 1:2-4). James encourages believers to be joyful when they go through little while times. He realizes they are good for us. They make us stronger. He understood that the thought of adversity being bad for us, was just a myth.

Myth #2: God will never give you more adversity than you can handle.

Pastors and counselors are known for encouraging people that God won't give them more than they can handle. They even back it up with Scripture: "No temptation has overtaken you that is not common to man. God is faithful, and he will not let you be tempted beyond your ability, but with the temptation he will also provide the way of escape, that you may be able to endure it" (1 Corinthians 10:13). They emphasize that it won't go "beyond your ability" and that you will escape or endure it. Their goal is encouragement. However, there is a problem. People are misquoting or misusing the verse. The context is temptation, not adversity.

God says He won't give us sin that we have

to say yes to. We can't blame God for putting us in a situation where we have to sin. In situations where we are tempted, He provides a way out. The topic is sin, not adversity.

The context is temptation, not adversity

If you think God won't give you more adversity that you can handle; then don't get in the lion's den. Don't enter the fiery furnace. Don't face the giant. For that matter, don't get married or have children because you are regularly in a battle too big for yourself. When Moses was fleeing the Egyptian army, facing the Red Sea, and leading a group of bellyaching Israelites; do you think he was faced with more than he could handle? Absolutely!

Moses, Daniel, Shadrach, Meshach, Abednego and David all faced adversities too big for their own strength. They couldn't handle it. But, they had a God who could handle an army, the sea, lions, fire and giants. God gave them more than they could handle. They gave it to God and He overcame the struggle.

If you can't handle a struggle, give it to the One who can.

Instead of misquoting 1 Corinthians 10:13, look at what Paul says in 2 Corinthians 12:7-10, So to keep me from becoming conceited because of the surpassing greatness of the revelations, a thorn was given me in the flesh, a messenger of Satan to harass me, to keep me from becoming conceited.

Three times I pleaded with the Lord about this, that it should leave me. But he said to me, "My grace is sufficient for you, for my power is made perfect in weakness." Therefore I will boast all the more gladly of my weaknesses, so that the power of Christ may rest upon me. For the sake of Christ, then, I am content with weaknesses, insults, hardships, persecutions, and calamities. For when I am weak, then I am strong.

Paul had a struggle, but God didn't remove it. He lived with the thorn in his flesh so that he would find strength in God, not himself. In God, I am strong. On my own, I am weak.

Paul says in Philippians 4:13, "I can do all things through him who strengthens me." The emphasis should not be on me. The emphasis should be on Him. I can do all things through Christ because He strengthens me. I can't do anything worthwhile on my own. However, I can do all things through Him.

These passages not only refute the myth that God won't give us more than we can handle, but also overturn the first myth that adversity isn't good for us. Paul found his strength when he was weak. The third myth is common and is often used to hold us in bondage through guilt.

Myth #3: Adversity always comes because of sin.

It is painful to hear pastors preach this garbage. This myth, although all too common, can be quickly defused through Scripture.

John 9:1-3 says, "As he passed by, he saw a man blind from birth. And his disciples asked him, 'Rabbi, who sinned, this man or his parents, that he was born blind?' Jesus answered, 'It was not that this man sinned, or his parents, but that the works of God might be displayed in him.'" The disciples saw a blind man and assumed he was blind because of sin. They assumed his adversity came because of sin. Jesus clearly says that it was not due to his sin or his parents' sin. The blind man's adversity came so that "the works of God might be displayed in him." Adversity can come in our lives so that our neighbors, friends and family can see God.

The life of Job also shows that the belief that adversity always comes because of sin is a myth. Job 1:1 says, "There was a man in the land of Uz whose name was Job, and that man was blameless and upright, one who feared God and turned away from evil." Job is described as blameless, upright, one who feared God and who turned away from evil. God makes it clear that Job was not going to enter the next stage of his life because of sin. In the next verses we see adversity hit him in financial loss and even in the death of his children. He was hit big time. Job's response is amazing: "Then Job arose and tore his robe and shaved his head and fell on the ground and worshiped. And he said, 'Naked I came from my mother's womb, and naked shall I return. The Lord gave, and the Lord has taken away; blessed be the name of the Lord'" (Job 1:20-21). Job realized God had a plan. He didn't beat himself up thinking he must have done something wrong. In the following

Job realized God had a plan

chapters, he doesn't let his friends discourage or defeat him into thinking he was being punished with adversity. Job 1:22 gives God's summary of Job's response: "In all this Job did not sin or charge God with wrong."

The story is told of a young man who went to his grandmother to vent. He explained to her how the world was beating him up. He spoke of things at work and home. Grandma faithfully listened. She always did. As she listened she grabbed three pots, put water in them, put them on the stove and turned on the heat. As the young man continues to whine, the water begins to boil. Grandma continues to listen as she throws a couple raw carrots into the first pot, puts an egg in the second pot and puts some coffee beans in the third pot. After listening a little while longer, she explains the meal. She tells her grandson that the water represents the world and the heat represents the adversity. She takes a carrot out and smashes it on a plate with her fork. She said when adversity comes it can break you to the point you are smashed. She then takes out the egg, runs it under cold water and peels it. She says adversity can make you hardened. Then she takes the third pot and pours it into a cup. She takes a drink of the coffee and says, "Or it can change the world." When our lives heat up, we have a decision on how to respond. Remember, God may want to change the world.

It has been said, "When you are ready to be a real Christian, not a Sunday morning Christian, but a real Christian who lives it all the time; you will be abundantly happy, you will be extremely fearless and you will always be in trouble."

Adversity is going to come. It isn't bad for us. We may not be able to handle it on our own. It probably isn't because of sin. Myths abound to distract us from the Lord and His Word. When the disciples asked, "Where are we going to celebrate the Passover?" Jesus told them to go into town and follow the man carrying the water. The unnamed man wasn't what was important; it was the water, the message. Follow the man who rightly carries the Word. In essence, when adversity comes, follow the Word.

Adversity will come. Remember the words of Lawnchair Larry, "Man can't just sit there."

Picture by Paul J Everett

"Try not to become a man of success, but rather try to become a man of value."

Albert Einstein

Chapter 11

What Am I?

Napolean Elvord is known for being a lot of things: Veteran, kidney patient, coffee lover and $14.3 million Wisconsin Megabucks winner. The strange thing is that Napolean didn't know he won. He didn't know he was a winner. The winning ticket was on his table at home for 3 days. Finally, he remembered to check the ticket, and he found out he won. He then took the winning ticket to the Wisconsin Lottery office and opted for the $10.2 million lump sum payment, which is $6.87 million after taxes. Napolean almost missed the fact that he was a winner.

What did he do next? Did he buy houses, cars and boats? No, he set the money aside to pay for a kidney transplant and plans to use some of the money to help other kidney patients. Fortunately, Napolean Elvord realized he was a winner.

All too often, Christians forget what they are. They start the day gloomy and avoid all light. They dwell in little while times because they feel defeated, useless and unimportant. Ephesians 1:1-7 gives seven aspects of the Christian's life. These seven items are medicine for when you feel in the dumps.

If you don't know what you are, you will miss out on what you are to do.

1. I am "Sainted"

Paul starts Ephesians 1:1-7 by saying, "Paul, an apostle of Christ Jesus by the will of God, To the saints who are in Ephesus, and are faithful in Christ Jesus." Paul writes to the saints in Ephesus. Be careful not to miss this. Most people think of saints as people from the past who lived nearly perfect lives (or at least no public sin), wore robes everywhere, performed a miracle or two, chanted and are now remembered through a statue decorated by pigeons. However, in the New Testament, a "saint" was the normal designation for a Christian. All Christians were referred to as saints. Once we have accepted the redemptive work of Jesus Christ, we are a saint. Did you realize you were a saint?

Once you become a saint of God, you are forgiven. You are forgiven for every sin ever committed. The guilt is gone. You are set free from the bondage of the world. The Greek implies that you are "set apart ones." God has set us apart, and we are called saints. Paul refers to saints from other locations too: Rome (Romans 1:7), Jerusalem (Romans 15:25), Corinth (1 Corinthians 1:2), Philippi (Philippians 1:1), Caesar's household (Philippians 4:22), Colossae (Colossians 1:2). Paul calls Christians saints. As a believer, you are a saint.

We need to celebrate being a saint. Remember

the old hymn, "When the saints go marching in"?

Oh, when the saints go marching in
Oh, when the saints go marching in
Lord, how I want to be in that number
When the saints go marching in

As believers and followers of Jesus Christ, we will be in that number. We will be one of the saints marching into the city of God.

Paul expands on this later in Ephesians when he says, "For through him we both have access in one Spirit to the Father. So then you are no longer strangers and aliens, but you are fellow citizens with the saints and members of the household of God" (2:18-19). Through Jesus Christ we have access to God. We are not aliens. We are not strangers. We are fellow citizens. We are saints. Later, in chapter 4 verses 11-12 Paul states, "And he gave the apostles, the prophets, the evangelists, the shepherds and teachers, to equip the saints for the work of ministry, for building up the body of Christ." Pastors are to equip and build up the people of the church, the saints.

Robert McCracken gives a timely reminder, "A man can be truly a saint in a factory as in a monastery, and there is as much need of him in the one as in the other." I am a saint of Jesus Christ wherever I am.

2.   I am "Graced"

Paul says in verse 2, "Grace to you and peace

from God our Father and the Lord Jesus Christ."
Paul gives the natural Greek and Hebrew greetings
in wishing grace and peace. He bestows grace on
believers. We are graced.

Grace is the unmerited, undeserved favor of
God. Paul makes it clear that God's grace is a gift:
"For by grace you have been saved through faith.
And this is not your own doing; it is the gift of God
(Ephesians 2:8)," and "Of this gospel I was made
a minister according to the gift of God's grace,
which was given me by the working of his power"
(Ephesians 3:7). God's grace involves salvation and
ministry. Paul goes on to say in 2 Corinthians 12:9
that God's grace gives power: But he said to me,
"My grace is sufficient for you, for my power is
made perfect in weakness. Therefore I will boast all
the more gladly of my weaknesses, so that the power
of Christ may rest upon me." This is the amazing
grace of God that can sustain us through our little
while times.

Mercy and grace are two different gifts of
God. Mercy is not getting what you deserve, while
grace is getting what you don't deserve. A simple
home situation can clarify the distinction. Imagine a
child disobeys and is suppose to get spanked twice.
(Now remember: Kids are like a canoe – they are
best steered with a paddle in the rear.) The first
spanking is justice. If the parent believes the lesson
has been learned and chooses not to give the second
swat, this is mercy. Deciding to go for ice cream
once everything has been settled is grace.

God calls us saints and has given us grace.

3. I am "Blessed"

Ephesians 1:3 continues the description of believers: "Blessed be the God and Father of our Lord Jesus Christ, who has blessed us in Christ with every spiritual blessing in the heavenly places." God has blessed us. We are blessed by God. It is who you are in Christ.

When you realize God is in control and that you are blessed, your life will be different. God blesses His followers.

Are you going through a little while time because of your stand for Christ? Stay strong. Scripture is clear that those who take one for the Lord, will be blessed:

- Blessed is the man who remains steadfast under trial, for when he has stood the test he will receive the crown of life, which God has promised to those who love him. James 1:12
- Behold, we consider those blessed who remained steadfast. You have heard of the steadfastness of Job, and you have seen the purpose of the Lord, how the Lord is compassionate and merciful. James 5:11
- But even if you should suffer for righteousness' sake, you will be blessed. Have no fear of them, nor be troubled. 1 Peter 3:14
- If you are insulted for the name of Christ, you

are blessed, because the Spirit of glory and of God rests upon you. 1 Peter 4:14

God has not forgotten us. He has blessed us. He has given us grace and called us saints.

4.   I am "Chosen"

Ephesians 1:4 says, "Even as he chose us in him before the foundation of the world, that we should be holy and blameless before him." We are set apart for God in order to reflect His purity. He chose us. He picked us. He wanted us.

Warren Wiersbe said, "This is the wonderful doctrine of election, a doctrine that we cannot fully explain but that we can fully enjoy." Why did God chose me? I don't know and can't fully explain it. I know I don't deserve it, but He chose me and ordained me to go.

Do you remember as a child wanting to be picked for a team? The suspense could be miserable. No one wanted to be picked last or worse yet, thrown aside. We all wanted to be picked.

1 Thessalonians 1:4 says, "For we know, brothers loved by God, that he has chosen you." That is such a simple, yet profound verse. Colossians 3:12 puts forth a challenge: "Put on then, as God's chosen ones, holy and beloved, compassionate hearts, kindness, humility, meekness, and patience." God chose us to a calling. He wants to make a difference in the world through us.

Unger's Bible Dictionary defines chosen as, "Singled out from others for some special service or situation." God chose us for a reason, for a purpose. Don't be part of the frozen chosen.

The key is celebrating who I am in Christ – how He sees me and how He knows me: that's who I am. I am a saint who is graced, blessed and chosen

.

5. I am "Adopted"

Ephesians 1:5 continues our description: "He predestined us for adoption as sons through Jesus Christ, according to the purpose of his will." God adopted us as His children. He not only chose us on His team, He made us family. We have been adopted into the family of God.

Under Roman law, an adopted son enjoyed the same position and privileges as a biological son. Today, adoption brings a brand new birth certificate. You are a child of God. You are a joint heir with Jesus Christ. God is your father.

Check out these two beautiful passages that describe our adoption by God:

Romans 8:14-17

For all who are led by the Spirit of God are sons of God. For you did not receive the spirit of slavery to fall back into fear, but you have received the Spirit of adoption as sons, by whom we cry, "Abba! Father!" The Spirit himself bears witness with our spirit that we are children of God, and if children, then heirs—heirs of God and fellow heirs with Christ, provided we suffer with him in order that we may also be glorified with him.

Galatians 4:4-7

But when the fullness of time had come, God sent forth his Son, born of woman, born under the law, to redeem those who were under the law, so that we might receive adoption as sons. And because you are sons, God has sent the Spirit of his Son into our hearts, crying, "Abba! Father!" So you are no longer a slave, but a son, and if a son, then an heir through God.

We often start prayer saying, "Dear Heavenly Father." Do we really comprehend and accept this treasure? God is my father. He adopted me. I am special because He calls me a saint, He gives me grace, He blesses me, He has chosen me and He even adopted me.

6.   I am "Made Accepted"

Paul continues, "To the praise of the glory of his grace, wherein he hath made us accepted in the beloved" (Ephesians 1:6 KJV). God made us accepted.

The Book of Philemon is only 1 chapter long, but it provides a very interesting story. Onesimus committed a crime against Philemon. Onesimus is put in jail. While in jail, he meets Paul and gives his life to Jesus Christ. Paul and Philemon are good friends. Paul has done a lot for Philemon. Once Onesimus is released, Paul writes to Philemon asking his friend to receive Onesimus as he would receive him: "So if you consider me your partner, receive him as you would receive me" (verse 17). Paul wanted to make Onesimus acceptable. Philemon would do anything for Paul, so Paul asks him to do it for Onesimus.

Through Jesus' work, He basically tells God to receive this saint "as you would receive me." Jesus has made us acceptable to God.

There are times that we may feel weird. We just don't feel like we fit in. We are convinced we are not accepted Just remember when no one wanted you, He accepted you. God accepted you.

Simple observation: Everyone is weird. If you are not weird, then you are weird because you are the only person not weird. However, even in our weirdness, God made us accepted.

7.   I am "Redeemed"

Finally in verse 7 Paul says, "In him we have redemption through his blood, the forgiveness of our trespasses, according to the riches of his grace."

A. Skevington Wood states in the Expositor's Bible Commentary that redemption has to do with the emancipation either of slaves or of prisoners. Some translations use the word "release." By derivation, the term also implies the payment of a ransom price. The price paid for man's redemption from bondage to sin was costly beyond measure. It was the very lifeblood of Christ Himself, poured out in death.

Basically, God was going through a shopping market. He took me from the bottom shelf and put me in His basket. He then went to the checkout counter and set me on the belt. The cashier picked me up, turned me over and scanned me. There was a price that had to be paid. God said, "I would like to redeem this one." The cashier said, "It will cost you your life." And He redeemed me. He paid the price in full.

We should celebrate because who we are in Christ. Galatians 3:13, "Christ redeemed us from the curse of the law by becoming a curse for us—for it is written, 'Cursed is everyone who is hanged on a tree.'" Our redemption, while free to us, was very costly. It cost Jesus His life. Romans 3:23-24 says, "For all have sinned and fall short of the glory of God, and are justified by his grace as a gift, through the redemption that is in Christ Jesus." We sinned. We fell short of God's standard, which is perfection. We couldn't pay the price to be released. So, Jesus did and gave it as a gift.

As Christians, we are sainted, graced, blessed, chosen, adopted, made accepted and redeemed.

Napolean Elvord almost missed out on realizing he had won the lottery. He is not the only one. Three winning tickets were purchased for the Maryland Mega Millions lottery worth $640 million. One of the three winners has yet to claim their prize. It is a shame to have access to so much and not tap into it.

Likewise, we as believers need to tap into what we are in Jesus Christ.

Picture by Lululemon Athletica

For I consider that the sufferings of this present time
are not worth comparing
with the glory that is to be revealed to us.

Romans 8:18

Chapter 12

"Have to"

Remember the saying, "The only thing you have to do is pay taxes and die"? Squabbles would take place over ideas like, "I don't have to die, the rapture might occur." Others would say, "I don't have to pay taxes; I can go to jail." We would argue over a silly phrase that was even quoted wrong. Ben Franklin actually said, "The only thing certain is death and taxes." However, this does lead to an interesting thought about what we actually have to do.

John chapter 4 gives one of the things Jesus said He had to do. John 4 is the story of Jesus' meeting with the woman at the well, whose life was a mess. This passage could be the motto or model for the church. The church should be for broken people. It should be a place where you come as you are and leave better than you entered. We need to stop giving the impression that people need to "clean up" before they come to church. People need to come to Jesus as they are, so He can help them, heal them. It is His love they need through the church, and through us.

We live in a broken world. Our families are

broken. A recent study found that more children

don't live with both natural parents than do. It has been known for too long that too many marriages are broken. Even ones that stay together can be hurting and lacking. The economical and political tones of our country leave us feeling broken. Ideally, the church has to rise to the occasion. However, too many churches are broken. People think numbers equal success. The Gospel is watered down or even neglected. The church becomes a feel good place. Broken people remain broken.

How did we get here?

How did this happen?

John 4:1-4 gives the setting for Jesus meeting the woman at the well, but also sets a philosophy that explains how some people end up in a little while time, and how they can start moving in the right direction:

Now when Jesus learned that the Pharisees had heard that Jesus was making and baptizing more disciples than John (although Jesus himself did not baptize, but only his disciples), he left Judea and departed again for Galilee. And he had to pass through Samaria.

Verse 1 explains that Jesus is being recognized as the Messiah, the Promised One. He is the answer to their problems (He was then and He is now). People identify with Him through baptism. They identify with the Messiah's death, burial and resurrection. Verse 2 clarifies that actually the disciples baptized while Jesus preached. Verse 3 lets it be known that Jesus left. Judea is like a state (i.e. Michigan), while Jerusalem is the most famous city. Jesus was going to head North to Galilee (in Michigan we would equate them to the Uppers, or people from the Upper Peninsula). All the disciples, but one, were from Galilee. The Galileans were known for being uneducated, woodsy people. They were the North people. Finally, verse 4 simply says that He "had to" (ESV) or "must needs" (KJV) pass through Samaria.

Jesus had to go through Samaria. This sounds innocent enough; however, typically a Jew would go around Samaria. They would avoid these people. They definitely didn't have to travel that way - there was an alternate route. But, Jesus had to pass through Samaria. Why?

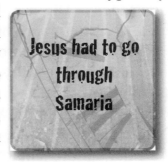

Some theologians think that Jesus was scared because the outskirts were too dangerous. They feel it was life and death. They are partially right. It was a life and death situation. It was eternal life and death for the woman at the well. Jesus wasn't afraid for His life; He was concerned for this lost, broken woman. He had to go through Samaria to talk with her. Jesus was about to transform her life and then that of a whole city.

Jesus "had to" go through Samaria. This introduces three categories for our lives: Have to, Need to, and Want to. Each of us evaluates decisions based on these three categories. Sometimes we place too much emphasis in one category, and it causes us problems.

The "Have to" category would contain a topic like work. We may not like work. We may dread going to work. But we have to go to work. The "Need to" category contains items like cutting the grass, cleaning the garage, washing the windows or vacuuming the house. It is not a life and death matter, and it probably won't get done today. The last category is the "Want to" area. We want to go shopping, fishing or golfing.

The American culture has been confused into thinking that all you should do is the "Want to" list. We feel we owe it to ourselves. We deserve to be happy. We need to watch out for Number One because no one else will. This is why our children, marriages, businesses, country and church are falling apart: People aren't willing to do what they have to do. They only focus on what they want to do.

If we feed the big dog, "Want to," too much, that big dog will eat us. We will destroy ourselves. Parents must raise their children understanding that there are some things that their children have to do. Hollywood even has great movie scenes of parents making their children eat their vegetables before they leave the table. If children ate just what they wanted to, they would get sick, be unhealthy and have rotten teeth. We make our children go to school. If children got to choose whether or not to go to school, no one would finish 4th grade.

Sometimes you have to do what you have to do because you have to.

Unfortunately, adults don't always follow their own instructions and live a life that is over saturated with "Want to." The average family lives on 108% of their income. The math clearly shows danger is coming. The average credit card debt per household with families who have credit card debt is $16,000. The world of "Want to" leads to self destruction. 2 Thessalonians 3:10 says, "For even when we were with you, we would give you this command: If anyone is not willing to work, let him not eat." You may not want to go to work, but you have to go. We need to be willing to do what we have to do.

There are some areas that we need to evaluate our response to. We need to place these items into one of the three categories: Have to, Need to, Want to.

1.   Do we Have to, Need to or Want to go to church?

Do we only go to church when we feel like it? Do we go to church as long as we feel it is meeting a need? Do we believe God desires us to go, so it becomes a priority in our lives?

Half of Americans would classify themselves as Protestant. They would acknowledge that they believe in the death, burial and resurrection of Jesus Christ. However, less than half of them go to church. If asked about church attendance, they would typically respond, "I know I need to be there." Yet, they don't go.

The typical mega church movement isn't helping the cause. They tend to target "Want to" believers. They strive on entertaining and putting on a show. Some churches are now even including tattoo parlors outside the sanctuary and holding MMA (mixed martial arts) fights to attract  crowds. They then preach a feel-good message that is politically correct and doesn't step on any toes. People leave believing since God loves everyone, they have no responsibilities. This environment of "Want to" totally ignores sin and its consequences.

Hebrews 10:24-25 says, "And let us consider how to stir up one another to love and good works, not neglecting to meet together, as is the habit of some, but encouraging one another, and all the more as you see the Day drawing near." The writer warns that people will neglect meeting together. People will habitually miss. Church won't be a priority for many, but we need to press on. We "Have to" go to church to encourage others in love and toward good works. We need to encourage each other. . We need relationships; first, with God Himself through Jesus Christ, and second, with fellow believers. Church is about relationships, not religion. We "Have to" go to church.

2. Do we Have to, Need to or Want to serve God?

There is a dangerous church philosophy being spread around: If we can just get everybody in the church to do something they want to do, then everything will be ideal. This sounds peachy, but there is no biblical basis for it.

When called by God, Moses responded by saying, "I don't want to go." God didn't then look for someone wanting to go. He said, "You have to go. I chose you." Moses bargained to have Aaron come along. He then followed God, not because it was fun or cool, but because he knew he "Had to."

Matthew 26:39-44 gives the greatest example of doing what you have to do:

And going a little farther he fell on his face and prayed, saying, "My Father, if it be possible, let this cup pass from me; nevertheless, not as I will, but as you will." And he came to the disciples and found them sleeping. And he said to Peter, "So, could you not watch with me one hour? Watch and pray that you may not enter into temptation. The spirit indeed is willing, but the flesh is weak." Again, for the second time, he went away and prayed, "My Father, if this cannot pass unless I drink it, your will be done." And again he came and found them sleeping, for their eyes were heavy. So, leaving them again, he went away and prayed for the third time, saying the same words again.

Jesus did not "Want to" go to the cross. Three times He asked His Father if there was another way. He passionately pleaded with God. Finally, He knew He "Had to" go. It was a matter of life or death, eternal life or death - for us.

In Luke 9:23, Jesus gives guidelines for following Him: "And he said to all, 'If anyone would come after me, let him deny himself and take up his cross daily and follow me.'" The challenge, command and even standard for following Christ starts in denying ourselves.

We have to step away from "Want to" and step up to "Have to." This is not saying that we will never want to follow Christ. Nor is it saying that we won't see the need to follow Christ. This challenge is in those times that we don't feel like it or see the value; it is then we still serve because we "Have to."

The ultimate goal of serving Christ is to  hear Him say, "Well done, good and faithful servant" (Matthew 25:21). This will only be said to those who went past their comfort zone and into a commitment mode. It is not about ability, but availability. Serving God is not always fun. We do it because it is right.

3. Do we Have to, Need to or Want to obey the Word of God?

The Jefferson Bible is a book by Thomas Jefferson where he cut and pasted the passages of Scripture that he wanted. The book is officially called, The Life and Morals of Jesus of Nazareth. Are we this bold? Do we ever just cut out those passages that are too convicting for us, the ones that make us uncomfortable?

If we feed the big dog "Want to" too often, he will eat us. He will destroy us. There are times we have to do what we have to do because we have to.

There is a battle between popular preaching and honesty. Remember, Jesus died on the cross for us because He had to. It was the only way we could be forgiven of our sins. During little while times, we should focus on what we "Have to" do and press on. In Philippians 3:12-14, Paul states, "Not that I have already obtained this or am already perfect, but I press on to make it my own, because Christ Jesus has made me his own. Brothers, I do not consider that I have made it my own. But one thing I do: forgetting what lies behind and straining forward to what lies ahead, I press on toward the goal for the prize of the upward call of God in Christ Jesus." We need to press on.

Christians "Have to" do what they "Have to" do.

Picture by Randy Willis

Weeping may tarry for the night,
but joy comes with the morning.
Psalm 30:5

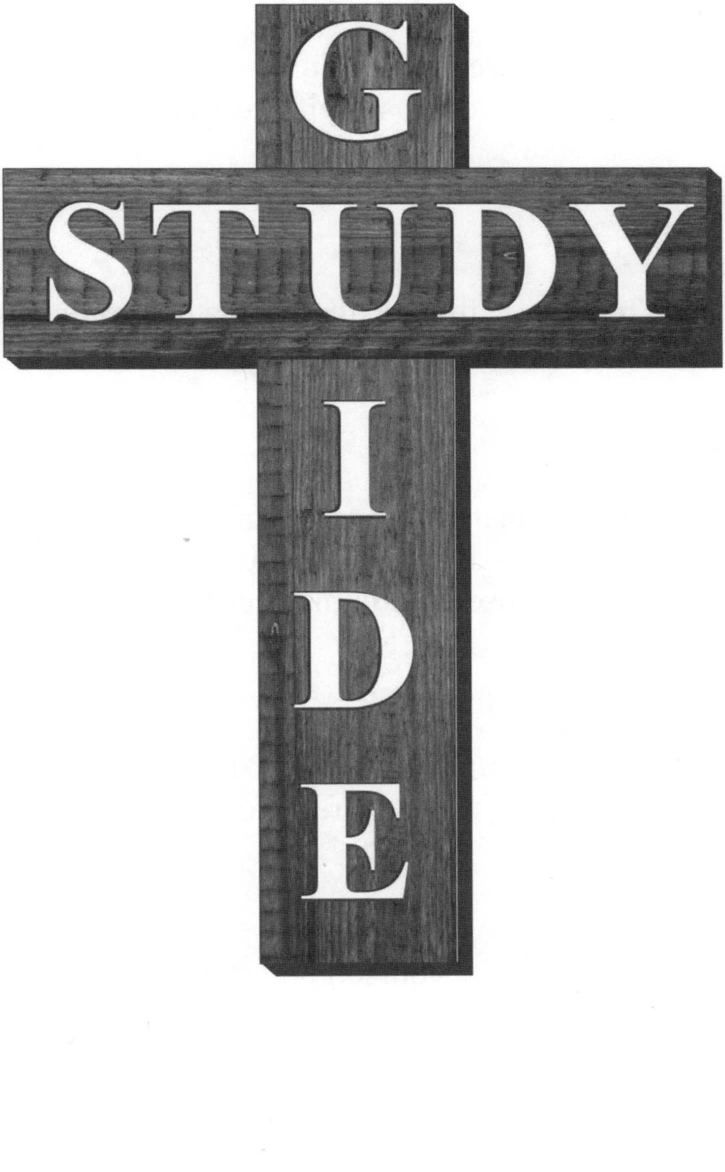
STUDY
GUIDE

Chapter 1

Bitter Sweet

1. Has there ever been a time in your life where you were just trying to figure out how to survive?

2. Why do you think Ruth made a commitment to stay with her mother-in-law?

3. Can you relate to Naomi? Has there been a time in your life where you have become bitter because of circumstances of life?

4. How will you begin to live "other" focused, rather than "self-centered" focused?

5. Make a list for yourself and start today.

Chapter 2

"Get Thee Up"

1. What does religion mean to you? What does a relationship with God mean to you?

2. Have you found that most of your little while times have come from your bad decisions?

3. Has whining really gotten you anywhere?

4. Where do you need to take responsibility? Who (or what) have you been blaming for what has happened in your life?

5. What part will you take in making a change for the good in your life, your home, your marriage and at work?

6. Get honest with yourself: Who are you
   pleasing with your life?

7. Remember the grace of God will take you
   places you thought you could never go.
   Make a list of things, or relationships, that
   you know need to be made right in your life.

Chapter 3

Two Strikes and You're Out

1. Have there ever been days in your life you wish you could go back and change?

2. Have you allowed the response of people around you to influence your behavior? Have they been your excuse why you react as you do?

3. Write a prayer of thanksgiving to God for blessing you despite your actions.

4. Give the "bitter-makers" to God. Write their name(s) here to remind yourself to pray for them.

5. Have you drunk from the Living Water, the water that gives you life?

If you would like to become a follower of God, just tell Him. Say, "God, I know I have done some pretty bad things and don't deserve Heaven, but actually deserve Hell. I am sorry. I want to change. I believe Your Son, Jesus, died for my sins. Although they buried Him, He rose again. I realize that Jesus offers eternal life to His followers. Today, I want to start following Him. Thank you.

Chapter 4

Left-Handed, Right-Minded

1. Which person are you?

   • I have the ability to overcome little while times.

   • I do not have the ability to overcome little while times.

2. Do you think your unique characteristic can't be used by God? (Did you forget who made you?)

3. Has the enemy tricked you into thinking you cannot be used by God because of your past? Are you limited because you are not like anyone else?

4. What little while time do you need to fight through that you have given up on?

5. Your Father in heaven wants to hear your
   frustrations. List them here and then get to
   work.

6. Are you stuck on the past? You must
   forgive, change what you can and forget
   what you can't change.

7. Write a list of 8 people you are hanging
   out with. Put a "P" next to the name if the
   person has a positive influence on you, and
   a "N" next to the negative influences. What
   are the results?

Chapter 5

Bottom Shelf Gospel

1. Do you panic when little while times come?

2. How will you change your thinking to realize that God has a plan for you during the little while times?

3. Looking back on a little while time, can you now see that God has used it to help someone else? How?

4. Have you felt like the shepherds? Did you think you were not good enough for the Son of God? Write a prayer of thanksgiving.

5. Have you looked down on people because they were not as "good" as you? Ask the Lord to give you His eyes. We need eyes to see people just as He sees them.

6. If you are going through a little while time right now, trust God to use you for His purpose. Write out 3 ways that you see that God can use this situation.

Chapter 6

Be Cool or a Fool

1. What do you think your response would be if you received the same horrible news that Horatio Spafford received?

2. Which are you?

   • I will listen to a problem so that a solution can be made.

   • I typically run away from problems.

3. Have you said things in anger that you regret? Do you tend to remain cool, or are you too often the fool?

4. Where do you seem to experience the most anger (home, church, school, work)?

5. Who tends to "make" you angry most often (spouse, children, boss, employee, self)? Lord to give you His eyes. We need eyes to see people just as He sees them.

6. What delayed action have you found to work best (count to 10, pray, leave for a moment)?

7. Is there something right now that you are angry about that you need to give over to God?

Chapter 7

String on My Finger

1. Where have you been when you have learned a life lesson?

2. How do you want people to remember you when you leave this life?

3. Write down 5 people who have had a positive impact in your life.

4. What characteristics about yourself are you glad are in the past?

5. Write a prayer of thanksgiving to God for sending the ultimate gift to you, His Son!

6. What do you think God has been doing recently for you upstream?

7. 7. Write down at least 3 things you know God has done for you in the past.

Chapter 8

Grapes – Giants – Grasshoppers

1. What is the condition of your soul? (Are you the older lady, older man or the little boy?)

2. Do you believe God's promises are real?

3. Have you allowed fear to stop you from going forward in life?

4. Do you find your perspective in life to be more positive or negative? Why do you think it is that way?

5. Do you think you have earned what you have, or are they blessings from God?

6. Have you ever stopped to really count your

blessings? List at least 5.

7. Where have you been disobedient to God

?
8. What obstacles in your life are you allowing to make you feel defeated?

9. Have you been living like a grasshopper?

Chapter 9

Dancing with God

1. What is stopping you from dancing with God? What will you do about it?

2. What do you live for? Is it something that is temporary?

3. What has happened in your life that is unexplainable, that you have realized only God could have orchestrated?

4. Do you ever feel shackled by life's disappointments? How have your responses been to those around you?

5. Are you living for Christ or for yourself? How will you practice dancing with God this week?

Chapter 10

Water Boy?

1. How much control does the easy chair and TV remote have over you? Be honest with yourself.

2. What does "playing religion" mean to you?

3. Have you ever thought God was punishing you because of the adversity in your life?

4. Who or what have you been following in times of adversity?

5. Has there been pain in your life? How do you think it can help someone else, or how do you think it can benefit you?

6. Have you allowed your problems to blind you so that you did not see God?

7. Have you been blaming past circumstances in your life for the decisions that you make now?

8. What adversity in your life do you need to give over to God?

9. When adversity comes, do you quickly beat yourself up, thinking you must have done something wrong?

10. What are you doing with the adversity in your life? Are you letting it smash you, make you hard or allowing it to develop you to change the world?

Chapter 11

What Am I?

1. Did you realize you are a saint if you have accepted the redemptive work of Jesus Christ? Was this a new concept for you? If so, why?

2. Write down a few times that you remember God's grace in your life.

3. You have been blessed! Bless somebody today. What will you do?

4. Did you know you were chosen by God? How does that make you feel?

5. What does being adopted by the heavenly Father mean to you?

6. Have you ever felt unaccepted by family or friends?

7. Have you put your trust in Jesus who paid the price in full for your redemption? If not, why don't you trust him right now?

Chapter 12

"Have to"

1. Is there brokenness in your life?

2. Do you think you need to "clean up" before you can go to God?

3. Has your "want to" category gotten you in trouble? Has it led you away from God?

4. Do you have to, need to or want to go to church?

5. Have you found yourself absent from church attendance? Why?

6. Do you have to, need to or want to serve God?

7. Is serving God on a convenience or commitment basis for you?

8. Do you have to, need to or want to obey the Word of God?

9. What has the Word of God been in your life?

10. Have you found yourself obeying some of the Word of God, but not all of it?

Acknowledgements

Pastor Jim and Doc Johnson are very blessed and thankful. They would like to specifically thank the following people:

Tom Gendich and Rochester Media for their support and direction.

Laura Hall and Sue Rowland for their attention to detail and editing expertize.

Brian Jamieson and Julius deChavez for their creative skills in graphic design.

Carole Combs for her insights and for preparing the study guide.

Angela Johnson whose idea sparked this whole project.